Something Special
The Inside Story of the Katherine West Health Board

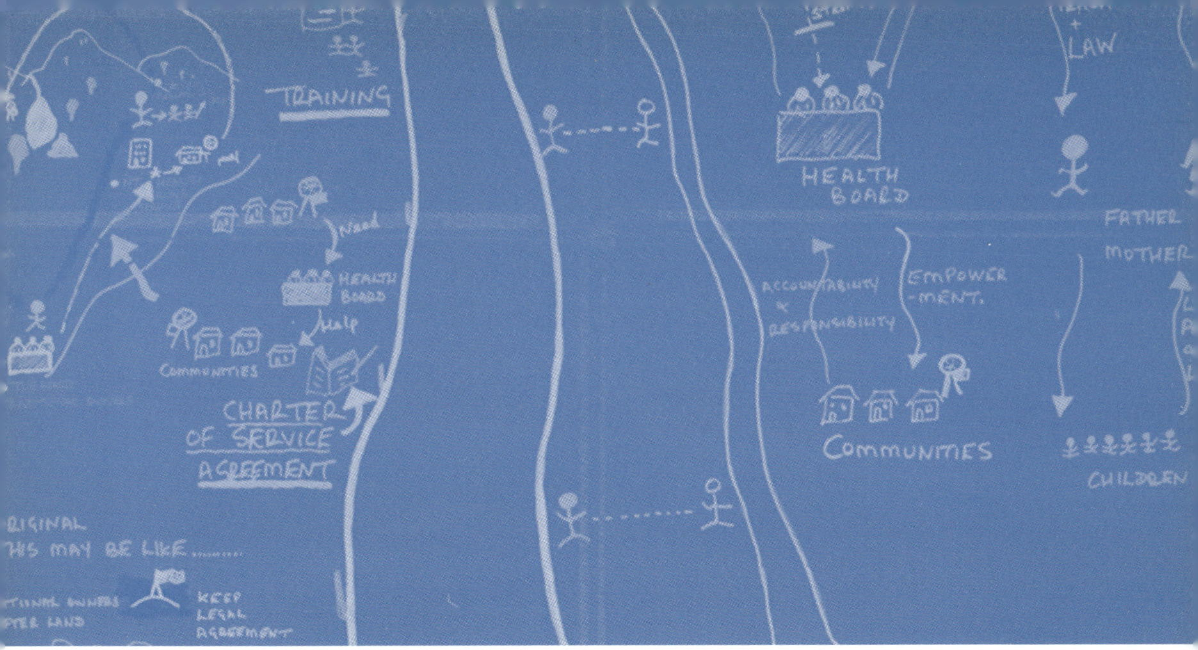

Something Special
The Inside story of the Katherine West Health Board

Katherine West Health Board

Aboriginal Studies Press

August 2003

Marion Scrymgour
(KWHB Director 1997–2001)

Jack Little
(KWHB Board Member from Bulla)

Willie Johnson
(KWHB Board Member for Latamano)

Joseph Cox
(KWHB Board Member from Doojum) KWHB Chairman

Norbert Patrick
(KWHB Board Member from Lajamanu)

Roy Harrington
(KWHB Board Member from Timber Creek)

First published in 2003 by Aboriginal Studies Press for the Australian Institute of Aboriginal and Torres Strait Islander Studies, GPO Box 553, Canberra, ACT, 2601.

© 2003 Katherine West Health Board

The Two Roads Poster reproduced with the kind permission of the Katherine West Health Board.

Apart from any fair dealing for the purpose of private study, research and criticism or review, as permitted under the Copyright Act, no part of this publication may be reproduced by an process whatsoever, withouth the written permission of the publisher.

National Library of Australia Catalouging-in-publication data:

Katherine West Health Board.
Something special : the inside story of the Katherine West Health Board.

Bibliography.
ISBN 0 85575 445 1.

1. Katherine West Health Board.
2. Aborigines, Australian - Medical care - Northern Territory. 3. Rural health services - Northern Territory. I. Title.

362.10899915

Contents

Preface	viii
Acronyms	x
Introduction	xi
Resistance, Part 1	1
Resistance, Part 2	19
Ideas for a Health Board	33
Early Days for the Board	57
Into the Live Phase	77
Taking Off	95
Beyond Coordinated Care	111

Preface

The original impetus for this booklet came from several individuals who had seen that what went on during the Katherine West Coordinated Care Trial was 'something special'.

The Health Board members had been interested in making sure other Aboriginal people and Governments heard their story. Governments saw the need for a resource which could help other newly-forming Aboriginal health boards. The compiler, Harvey Creswell, had been a Policy Officer at the Katherine West Health Board, and put the document together while a fulltime post-graduate student, flying back and forth between Sydney and Katherine to tape and consult. As it turned out, the ideal methodology, involving scientifically designed survey techniques and elaborate manipulation of data, was not possible. The reality is that it was a case of catching people 'opportunistically', taking a tape recorder on long trips from one community to another, only to find the relevant people had moved on to another community. So, in a haphazard fashion, most of those involved in the early days of the Health Board were tracked down, and gave their time generously.

Then, in the middle of the research, an election was called in the Northern Territory and Marion was endorsed as the Australian Labor Party candidate for the seat of Arafura. Suddenly her time became very scarce, and plans for in-depth taped conversations between Marion, Board members and Harvey had to be put off as Marion gave priority to campaigning. Nevertheless, there were long taped conversations between Marion and Harvey, which for Marion acted as 'debriefings' after four hard years—at last she was getting it all off her shoulders. From the interviews, key issues and events were identified and documentation about them sought in the KWHB's files.

Looking at the interview material, it was apparent that those involved saw the Katherine West story as part of their life's story. It was a part of the dramatic changes experienced by the generation which had known truly hard times. Now, it seemed, the pendulum of history was swinging in another direction. For that reason it was necessary to situate the Katherine West story in the context of the region's overall history.

For all these reasons, this is not an objective scientific study; it is a story told from a particular perspective.

Acknowledgement is gratefully made of the help given by all the people who were interviewed for this project. Thanks are also due to the Northern Land Council, which granted access to historical material. A small grant from Commonwealth Department of Health and Aged Care made research for the project possible.

It must be emphasised, however, that the views and opinions expressed in this booklet are those of the Katherine West Health Board. They are not necessarily the views or opinions of either the Commonwealth Department of Health and Ageing or of the Northern Territory Department of Health and Community Services.

Acronyms

AACAP ATSIC-Army Community Assistance Program

AHW Aboriginal Health Worker (in the Northern Territory, an Aboriginal person trained to provide a certain level of professional health care, with an emphasis on cultural appropriateness).

AMSANT Aboriginal Medical Services Alliance Northern Territory (the peak body representing Aboriginal community-controlled health services in the NT)

ATSIC Aboriginal and Torres Strait Islander Commission

CCTIS Coordinated Care Trials Information System

DHAC Commonwealth Department of Health and Aged Care

KWCCT Katherine West Coordinated Care Trial

KWHB Katherine West Health Board Aboriginal Corporation

MBS Medical Benefits Scheme or Medicare (the 'universal' health insurance scheme of the Commonwealth Government).

NLC Northern Land Council

OATSIH Office of Aboriginal and Torres Strait Islander Health Services (a part of the Commonwealth Department of Health and Aged Care)

PBS Pharmaceutical Benefits Scheme (a Commonwealth Government scheme which subsidises the price paid by consumers for pharmaceutical drugs)

THS Territory Health Services (a Department of the Northern Territory Government)

Introduction

> **The hardest concept is to implement health in a community development framework...**
> *Marion Scrymgour*
>
> **the Trial has already brought about important positive changes in the delivery of health services to the region. The results can be seen in terms of greater Aboriginal control of health services, increased resources, increasing emphasis on preventative services, and more effective clinical practices. These changes, if sustained, should lead to improved health outcomes in the future.**
> *Local Evaluation, Final Report*

In late 2001 the Katherine West Coordinated Care Trial (KWCCT) officially wound up, not long after the departure of the foundation Director of the Katherine West Health Board Aboriginal Corporation (KWHB), Marion Scrymgour. The KWHB had become an established feature of the Aboriginal health landscape in the Northern Territory, its ongoing status proving the proposition that positive change in Aboriginal health is possible, given the right conditions.

Since 1997 the KWHB had been doing its best to fill the primary health care needs of all the residents—both Aboriginal and non-Aboriginal—of a vast Region covering some 162,000 square kilometres of rolling bush and desert country on the western side of the Northern Territory.

In the judgement of all those involved in the KWCCT it had been a great success. For the two governments involved—the Commonwealth and the Northern Territory—the risk of committing large amounts of money to an untried experiment had paid off. For those living in the small communities and cattle stations scattered across the Region, the level of health servicing had improved to an extent they had not foreseen. For the staff of the KWHB, including Marion, pride in being part of a unique experiment was palpable. And for the elected members of the KWHB's governing Board, the fact that their commitment and hard work had produced results which all the world could now see showed that Aboriginal people could throw off the paternalism and negative stereotypes so pervasive in their childhoods and throughout the lives of their parents and grandparents.

The changes which took place over the course of the KWCCT had been profound:

- An elected Board of Aboriginal people from communities in the Region had been formed to take over many of the decision-making responsibilities for health servicing previously held by the Northern Territory Government.

- The Northern Territory Government had agreed to pay to the KWHB that money which it would have otherwise spent providing clinical and public health services to the residents of the Region.

- Additional health service funds had been injected into the Region, as the Commonwealth Government acted on the recognition that under the Medicare and Pharmaceutical Benefits Schemes Aboriginal people—particularly those living in remote areas far from doctors and pharmacies—were able to access only a small fraction of the Medicare funding accessed by non-Aboriginal Australians.

The Commonwealth had 'cashed out' the entitlements of the Region's residents to these schemes at the average Australian utilisation rate of $536 per person per year, and paid this to the KWHB.

- Under a tripartite Legal Agreement between the KWHB, the Northern Territory Government and the Commonwealth Government, the elected Board could then choose to either purchase health services from a health service provider or provide the services itself, using the funds pool formed from the contributions of the NT and Commonwealth Governments. The Board had discretion regarding its preferred mix of health services, within limits.

This was a potent mix : a transfer of power and responsibility from whitefella governments to a group of grassroots-oriented Aboriginal people, combined with a significant increase in the funds available to be spent. And all in the context of a Region with a history dominated by racist exploitation and cruelty. The stakes were high, and all concerned were determined to make this 'experiment' work.

Most had thought that the story of the KWHB started in 1997. But it did not. It started at least one hundred years earlier. The Board members of the KWHB have always seen their situation—and the situation of the KWHB—in a historical context of oppression and lack of a 'say' in their own futures. They grasped an opportunity in 1997 so strongly precisely because they had not had such opportunities in the past.

This is the story of 'Kath West'.

Resistance — Part One

> **The primary fact which philanthropists must accept is that the Aborigines regard the land as theirs, and that the intrusion of the white man is a declaration of war, and the result is simply 'survival of the fittest' ... occupation of the country for pastoral purposes and peaceable relations with the native tribes are hopelessly irreconcilable.**
> *Government Resident 1887, (Berndt & Berndt, p. 6)*

> **One cannot run both cattle and blacks on the one property, and I presume the cattle come first...**
> *Manager, Newry Station, 1937 (Riddett, p. 142)*

The reactions of the Ngarinman, Ngaliwurru, Bilinari, Miriuwung-Gadjerong, Gurindji., Warlpiri, Wuli, Mudbara and Wardaman peoples who sighted white men and cattle first entering their country in the 1880s and 1890s established a pattern of resistance repeated at various intervals over the course of the century. In this pattern, the various actors played out remarkably reliable stereotypes. Neglect and cruelty—to both country and people—were the hallmarks of white settlers. Tenacity and resistance—both active and passive—characterised the reactions of Aboriginal people. And governments combined subservience to foreign investors with home-grown development fantasies.

It is not the intention of this document to present many statistics. Rather, it is the quality of the encounters—health and otherwise—which shall be emphasised throughout. Nevertheless, there is a need to give at least some quantitative information to back up our generalisations. And for what went on in the period up to the mid-20th century, one set of numbers is more than adequate. When whitefellas entered the country which later became Victoria River Downs Station (VRD), the Aboriginal population was conservatively estimated at 4,200. At the first census taken on VRD, 55 years later, it was 187 (Rose 2000, p. 7).

Within that short period, around 90% of the population had been wiped out.

Within the broad themes of cruelty, resistance and official neglect, particular individuals occasionally stood out by breaking from the stereotype. Several white pastoralists (such as Reg Durack of Amanbijdi station) were notable for the respect and kindness shown to their Aboriginal employees. Several government officers (particularly some Patrol Officers) tried to remedy the neglect and cruelty shown to Aboriginal people. On the odd occasion, governments—notably those of the Australian Labour Party—made efforts to stand up to those destroying the land and people. But in the overall sweep of history, such individual efforts had little impact. In the end it was Aboriginal people who, after waiting for others to act, had no choice but to take decisive action themselves.

But this is jumping forward in time.

The legendary drover Nat Buchanan was the first outsider to assert residence rights in the Region when he took up Wave Hill Station in 1883, bringing cattle on lengthy overland drives from Queensland. He was followed shortly after by the Duracks and several others who leased adjoining properties. Three decades later, two large British meat companies, Vesteys and Bovril, bought out Wave Hill and Victoria River Downs (VRD) Stations. These were soon expanded into massive properties. By the end of the 1930s Wave Hill Station covered about 27,700 sq km and VRD some 32,800 sq km. A major cattle industry had begun.

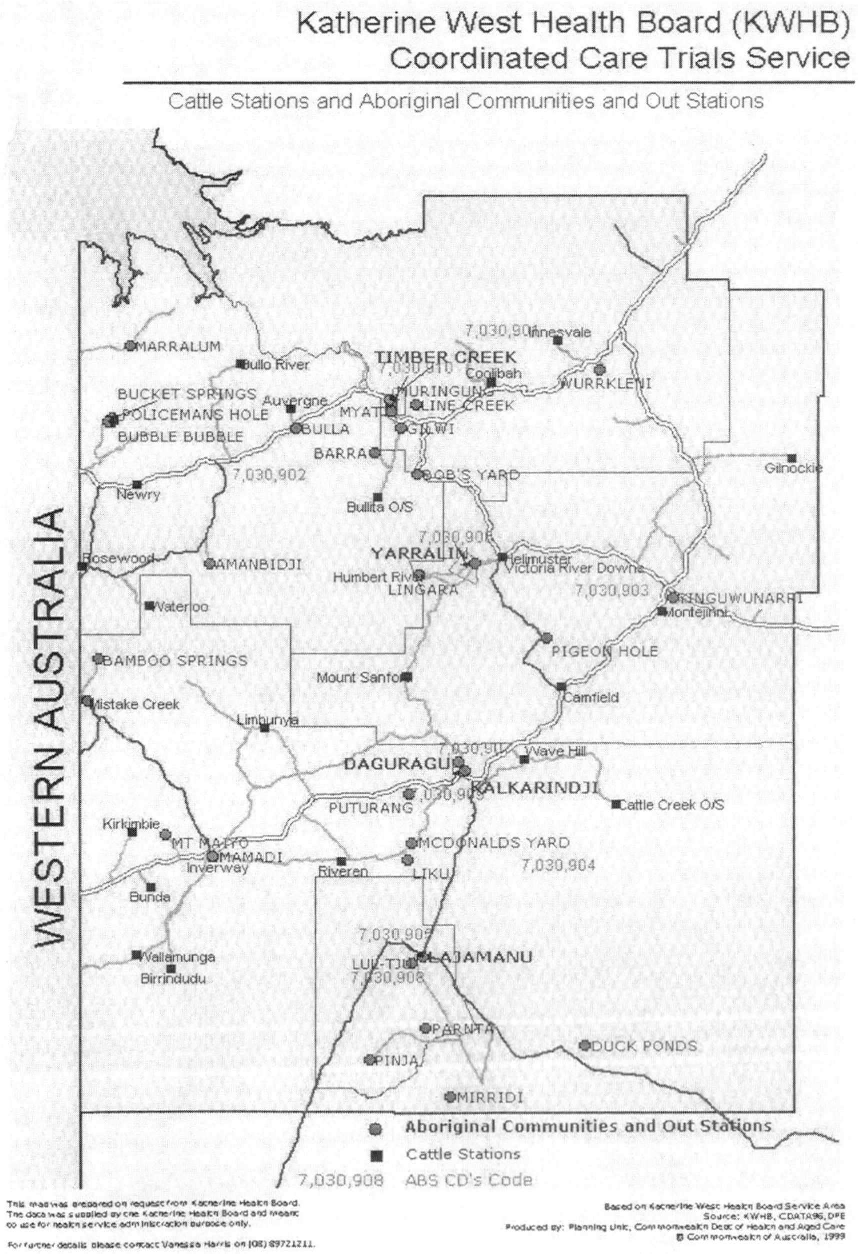

Katherine West Health Board (KWHB) Coordinated Care Trials Service

Cattle Stations and Aboriginal Communities and Out Stations

Map of Pastoral Leases

Of course, living on the country now covered by these stations were Aboriginal people. Never considered by the early pastoralists to have any rights of residence or ownership, if they wanted to stay on their own country they had little choice but to capitulate or fight. Most fought.

Early on, some of the settlers lives came under direct threat. Johnny Durack was fatally speared on Rosewood Station in 1886. Thomas Hardy died from a spear on Auvergene Station in 1889 and in 1890 a traveller through the Region was speared travelling up the Baines River. A policeman was fatally speared in 1893 in Rosewood Station country.

These were isolated events, however, with most Aboriginal action focusing on animal rather than human targets—though this did not make the early pastoralists any less fearful of or frustrated by the Aborigines, and there are numerous accounts of whitefellas complaining of their difficulties.

> **The myalls made themselves obnoxious by spearing horses and cows**
> *(Northern Land Council 1984)*
>
> **Blacks *very* hostile… we have held no communication with the natives at all except with a rifle**
> *(Northern Land Council 1984)*

The standard response to such attacks was to initiate 'punitive parties', and in places whole groups of Aboriginal people were summarily shot by both police and pastoralists. Such accounts by whitefellas are so numerous and candid that there is no doubt that many hundreds of Aboriginal people were murdered over the course of two or three decades. In some locations, whole language groups were entirely wiped out—the Karangpurru people, for instance, experienced a population loss of more than 99% - from 500 to 2. (Rose 1991, p. 78)

While there are many accounts by whitefellas of such frontier clashes, and of their views, what do we know of Aboriginal views ? Almost nothing, of course, by way of direct comment at the time. But the rich tradition of oral history fostered over the years meant that all Aboriginal people were aware of the starkness of the conflict. Many decades later a Mudbara man outlined what all his people have known for a long time :

> **... the white man stole our father's land from us. The fact that it was our fathers' land didn't matter to the white man when he came in from a far country and brought houses, horses and cattle. It wasn't his land but he's still there, living on our land. First of all we just let him do it, we just watched what the white men were doing. Then the white men shot some of my grandfathers, some of my fathers, and some of my uncles, even though they were doing nothing wrong. Then they took away the women from the old men. Then they came for younger Aboriginals and put them to work. The fact that we had not harmed them didn't make any difference. They came looking for a fight and killed us, because they wanted our land. 'We'll have to spear them' said the old men. They attacked the white men. The Aboriginals threw the old-fashioned spears with stone heads, but the**

> white men fired guns back. They shot them down, poor things, and cleared the Aboriginals off the land. When they had taken away the land, they called it their own land, just as if they had inherited it from their fathers. They brought in their houses, horses, cattle and barbed wire. The land had belonged to the Aboriginals, but now the white man thought the Aboriginals' land was theirs. They had shot the Aboriginals off their own land all along the Victoria River and at every spring, although the Aboriginals were doing no wrong. They divide it up among themselves. 'That's mine' the white men would say to each other. 'That's my block'.
> *(Northern Land Council 1979, p. 93)*

Many particularly dramatic conflicts occurred at waterholes. Pastoralists, of course, needed them to water cattle and horses, not only draining the water which bush-dwelling Aboriginal people relied on for life, but also polluting any water which remained. It has been pointed out that the "recurrent spearing of cattle, without also exploiting them as a food source, could well be seen in terms of attempting to defend the waterholes from further destruction" (McConvell, quoted in Riddett).

Overt and direct Aboriginal resistance continued well into this century. In 1929 a policeman reported that "The bush aboriginals appear to be practically out of hand" (Riddett), and other accounts point to the problems which pastoralists had with 'bush blacks' killing cattle until well into the 1940s and 50s.

During this time, however, Aboriginal people were increasingly showing their usefulness to the pastoralists as labour. Indeed, they were the only available labour: everyone knew, not least of all Vesteys, that "if the Aboriginal was taken away the whole thing would collapse." (Secretary of the Northern Agency (Vesteys), quoted in Northern Land Council 1987, p 15).

In recognizing the utility of Aboriginal labour while refusing to provide humane working conditions, companies such as Vesteys were of course setting the scene for their own long-term demise. The lack of logic was breathtaking. On the one hand, in order to establish the pastoral properties, traditional small-group nomadic society had been decimated. On the other hand, it was expected that the Aboriginal labour force, now living in large sedentary groups in alienated country, could maintain their traditional lifestyles to such an extent that the colonisers were not responsible for the provision of food, clothing or sanitary living conditions.

The actual process whereby Aboriginal people came to work for the pastoralists was not straightforward. In reality, unrestrained slaughter of those Aborigines who did not readily submit was not quite as feasible during the 20th century as it had been in the 19th century. The sparseness of the white population, thinly scattered throughout a huge region ; the fact that Vesteys and Bovril left huge areas of their holdings in an 'undeveloped' condition ; and the strategic existence of inaccessible 'sandstone country' to which people could retreat, all left the way open for some groups of Aborigines to maintain a partial degree of independence.

Many were undoubtedly forced to come into the pastoral stations or face violence and likely death (McConvell, quoted in Riddett, p.130). Some came in voluntarily, initially lured by a liking for tobacco—building an addiction so strong as to temporarily reconcile groups with a history of conflict, such as Gurindji and Warlpiri, to working together. (Read and Japaljarri). Some came in to make contact with relatives, others from curiosity to learn about *gardiya* ways.

Some stations found it extremely difficult to recruit and hold Aboriginal employees, depending on whether or not they were prepared to tolerate a minimal degree of Aboriginal social organisation. At various times in the 1920s and 30s, stations such as Bullita, Auvergne and Newry had repeated problems holding Aboriginal labour, a situation which the local policemen put down to the fact that "aboriginals will not remain contented, nor will they come looking for work voluntarily if they are not allowed to form a camp, and keep their other tribal relatives with them" (quoted in Northern Land Council 1987), and to the proximity of other stations where conditions were slightly more tolerable. The significance of these situations was that Aborigines tried to maintain a partial degree of independence: among themselves they never accepted the view that they were *always* "… slaves, ruled by the whip and harsh words: and that *always* "the whites had the first and final say." (Cockburn-Campbell, quoted in Northern Land Council 1987)

The persistent difficulties of the pastoralists in holding their Aboriginal labour under all circumstances is testimony to a continuing resistance by Aboriginal people in the face of such strong exploitation. In reality, Aboriginal people moved in and out of the pastoral industry and from one station to another in response to the relative severity of working conditions and their cultural needs. It was increasingly hard to live off the land, but life on cattle stations was often worse.

The issue was not just a matter of poor health : it was a matter of whether Aboriginal people in the region would survive at all. Extinction could easily have happened. Of the 187 Aboriginal people on VRD in 1939, only 12 were children. (Rose 2000, p. 7). Somehow, some survived, and remembered.

> **During the worst years, people saw most of their children die, or had them wrenched from their arms to be taken to institutions. Sick people were taken away, and those with leprosy were permanently consigned to quarantine islands. In terrible pre-dawn raids their private parts were inspected for signs of venereal disease, their children and sick people grabbed, their dogs shot. Through it all, they sought to maintain the knowledge of self, society, and cosmos in which their essential identity was based. They held on in the hopes that at some future day they would be free. And they maintained a covert resistance so that when that day came there would be Aboriginal people who knew who they were, what traumas they had survived, where they belonged and what was incumbent upon them.**
> *(Rose 2000, p. 20)*

The legacy of this still confronts the Katherine West Health Board.

And what of governments during this time? In 1911 responsibility for administration of the NT changed from the South Australian Government to the Commonwealth. This, however, did not bring any benefits to Aboriginal people. In some ways, the Canberra administration showed itself to be even more blind to the aspirations and basic human rights of remote Aboriginal people than had the pastoralists of the NT. National politicians, with little idea of the realities of bush life or of conditions in the NT, continually espoused the need for 'development' in the far North, mostly as a security bulwark against an Asian invasion. Parliamentary debates before the Second World War repeated the same themes, over and over in a circular fashion. And in these debates, the focus was solely on the needs of white Australia— Aboriginal Australia simply did not figure in their plans in any way whatsoever. This blindness was based on development fantasies rather than on any acceptance of genuine responsibility for the country and people they were governing. Ironically, in giving huge pastoral companies virtually free reign in the name of 'development', the Commonwealth Government allowed Vesteys and Bovril to effectively block genuine development in the Region for many decades.

This absentee (and subsidised) ownership of massive tracts of the NT provided Vesteys and Bovril with the opportunity to simply treat land and people as they pleased. And if the remoteness of Canberra resulted in little interest by politicians in the reality of conditions in the NT, the distance between the London boardrooms of these companies and their cattle properties in Australia meant even more degradation for those living and working on these properties.

> **By the late 1930s it was obvious that (Vesteys) had been irresponsible in their management of the country, impractical in their development of station infrastructure and quite ruthless in denying their Aboriginal labour proper access to basic human rights, viz, a living wage and adequate, hygienic living conditions. They were not alone in these practices, Bovril, owners of VRD, shared the same criticism but Vesteys were probably the worst in**

> treatment of Aboriginal labour and second only to Bovril in mismanagement of natural resources.
>
> *(Riddett, p. 139)*

Health services in the Region during the pre-World War II years were of course minimal. Nursing sisters from the Australian Inland Mission based at VRD from 1923 to 1939. Their role was both medical and social, in a Region with almost no white women, and limited largely to providing services for the white settlers.

Despite a lack of formal records, there is little doubt that introduced diseases had been widespread in the Region right from the early days. A policeman recorded in 1927 that there had been "several deaths amongst the Bush Aboriginals during the epidemic of colds early in the quarter" and in 1928 the list of illnesses of Aboriginals taken to Darwin included yaws, granuloma, gonorrhea, leprosy, discharging ears and unknown skin diseases in and around the mouth. (Northern Land Council 1984)

There were numerous reports of leprosy and malaria in the Region over the decades, with Sister Kettle speculating that there was "ample scope" for the Chinese cooks and gardeners at Wave Hill to introduce leprosy and tuberculosis to the Aborigines. (Kettle 1991).

In the poor living conditions, trachoma became commonplace. In 1944, of 140 people examined by the Army in the Victoria River area, 11 were blind in both eyes and an additional 13 blind in one eye. (Kettle 1991 Vol 1, p. 316).

While neglect and cruelty undoubtedly predominated, the attitude of white society towards the Region's Aboriginal population was not entirely negative. Individual Patrol Officers tried to draw the authorities attention to the fact that

> the natives on cattle stations have no future.
> They are at the mercy of the cattle owners
> and stockman ... and cattle station staff
> have, with very few exceptions, little mercy...
> The result of their policy has been a
> decreasing native population and stagnation
> for the natives that remain on their holdings.
> *(quoted in Northern Land Council 1987)*

Neither were all pastoralists uniformly oppressive. In the early 1950s Reg Durack built the first houses for his Aboriginal stockmen and their families, Patrol Officer Evans reporting that they were "taking a keen interest in their huts and keeping them in a tidy manner" (quoted in Northern Land Council 1987) and later that decade Sister Kettle reported that adequate supplies of good quality bread and beef were issued three times a day to workers, pensioners and children. Cows were also milked daily, with skim milk given to the children." (in Northern Land Council 1987, p. 20)

Overall, however, the situation was as described by the well-known anthropologists, Ronald and Catherine Berndt, when they made a detailed survey of conditions in the mid-1940s. Vesteys, originally supportive of the survey on the basis that it would help them identify ways for them to solve their problem of a low Aboriginal birthrate and diminishing labour supply, did nothing to respond to its conclusions :

> ... the diet was unsatisfactory and
> inadequate both in type and in quantity, and
> was obviously insufficient to maintain a
> reasonable standard of health ... Continued
> undernourishment of local people over a

long period, helped out by only small quantities of bush food, must surely have been to a large extent responsible for a low birthrate situation. This was coupled with minimal sporadic medical attention ... Resistance to disease was diminished because of the poor diet, so that the tendency was for Aborigines to succumb readily to infection and make only a slow recovery...

No encouragement was given to Aborigines, either children or adults, to change the patterns of hygiene and sanitation that had been reasonable under semi-nomadic conditions ... No latrines of any kind were provided. Particularly in hot weather and where the camp (as at Wave Hill) was both large and stationary, the effects were exceedingly unhealthy, and a source of current and future infection.

Supplies of drinking water and washing water close to stations were irregular, with no moderately secure permanent source ...

No adequate shelters were provided for the use of station employees (or other Aborigines) during the wet season except such as they had themselves put together in their spare time from odd scraps of material. Consequently no training or encouragement was given to children and young adults in the construction, use or care of permanent dwellings...

Working conditions, even at their best, offered virtually no choice to the Aborigines concerned. The dominating feature was that they had to fit into the system without openly challenging it... Aboriginal people were regarded as one of the natural resources of the country, whose purpose in life was to serve the needs and desires of Europeans ... they had no appeal against any injustices to themselves or to their families ; and they were supposed to be at their employer's disposal at all hours of the day and night...

In remuneration for their labour they received the minimum of food, clothing, tobacco and so on, the cost of these being cut as much as possible to save expense. Their families were not adequately fed or provided for ; and ... they were continually saving small portions of food from their own meagre rations in order to supplement the supply of close relatives. This fact, together with the unsatisfactory nature of their diet, decreased their energy, health and working capacity...

No educational facilities of any kind were provided on the pastoral stations, or... desired for Aborigines by Europeans in the region at that time. Any reference we made to the subject was greeted with intense and

> frank hostility. To the local Europeans it was unthinkable that there should be any departure from the existing state of affairs ...
>
> Underlying the structure of the situation was a state of mutual intolerance and hostility between the two ethnic groups. This could be manifested openly by most Europeans. Among Aborigines it was latent and had to be carefully concealed... This foundation of suspicion and dislike was increased by the Europeans' determination to obtain useful labour and physical satisfaction, and to maintain their own prestige. On the part of Aborigines it was sustained by fear, and at the same time by a desire to obtain introduced food and material benefits...
> *(Berndt and Berndt, p 217-220)*

Aboriginal people—as anyone would—resisted this treatment as best they could. But to whom could they turn ? Isolated, with no knowledge of any government down south supposedly looking after their interests, and with the NT Department of Native Affairs having no influence whatsoever on what happened in the region, passive resistance was all that was possible.

> We couldn't, we didn't have any help behind (no-one to back us up). You know, we tried, but sort of frightened for—Aboriginal people (were) too frightened he might get shot. Like all my grandfa got shot before. That kind of law ; they were frightened ... (They thought) : 'Long as you can look after the

> land. Keep the place, right thing … . We
> might do something more sometime. We
> might turn the law someday. Any year's time.
> *(Riley Young Winpilin, in Rose 1991, p. xxi)*

But passively resist they did: refusal to consistently supply labour was one form of this. The low birthrate was another, as Aboriginal women limited family size in response to conditions. The dissatisfaction ran strong and deep, and it was not solely about the poor living conditions: it was grounded in the complete lack of appreciation of their worth as human beings.

Resistance — Part Two

> **These are a group of people of astonishing stamina and tenacity. They are among the incorruptibles. They are level-eyed people who demand the attention of our conscience.**
> The Australian, *26 June 1*

> **Tommy Vincent told Lord Vestey "You can keep your gold. We just want our land back."**
> *Hobbles Danayarri, in Rose 1991*

That war and its aftermath heralded big changes in the western pastoral regions of the NT. Although the conditions described by Berndt in his 1944 survey persisted on the prorperties controlled by Vesteys, Aboriginal people from the region also came to work in the big Army camps set up to the East during the War. Here they worked set hours, received decent food and had access to such fundamentals as showers, housing and latrines. Their use and appreciation of these facilities provided a clear demonstration of the needs ignored on the pastoral properties:

> **On the central western pastoral stations we had been assured that Aborigines did not want and would not use, at least not properly, taps, showers, latrines and other amenities so that there was no point in our recommending these. The Army settlements provided an excellent case study in that respect, confirming our opinion.**
> (Berndt and Berndt, p. 21)

But it was more than just a demonstration of practicality—it was a demonstration of equity and justice : there were rules which applied to everyone, with Aboriginals generally working under the same conditions as non-Aboriginals. So their self-respect was enhanced—and those Aboriginal people who had worked in the Army camps spread this word among those back on the pastoral properties. The talk had started.

In the provision of health services to residents of the western pastoral region, the immediate post-War period saw important opportunities squandered by the Commonwealth Government. The World Health Organisation had come into being, and the notion of rural health centres in underdeveloped countries—providing what would come to be called primary health care—was increasingly advocated. Officially, responsibility for control of health services in the NT had come under the Commonwealth Department of Health back in 1939 and after the War recommendations were made to that Department by Army doctors and others who knew what was needed in such remote areas. But they were all ignored, the Canberra-based Director-General of Health refusing to take responsibility for health services in the NT beyond the provision of four hospitals, a leprosarium and an Aerial Medical Service (Kettle 1991, Vol 2, p.65).

And so during the 1950s and 60s a small number of dedicated individuals did their best to provide some degree of health service to the remote regions. The first-ever dental survey of the cattle stations in the Victoria River area took place only in 1950. The first Medical Survey doctor in the NT was appointed in 1951, though it was not until the late 1950s that there were regular medical visits to cattle stations. Nursing sister Ellen Kettle travelled heroically—there is no other word—to most remote settlements, working always under enormously difficult conditions. She writes of the high prevalence in the 1950s of hookworm, trachoma, and tuberculosis at the newly-established Hooker Creek (Lajamanu), and of trachoma and dire infant nutrition problems at Wave Hill and VRD. Given the history and the conditions described by Berndt and others, such problems come as no surprise. The appalling situation which these few frontline health staff were trying to address is no more effectively illustrated than by the Aboriginal known infant mortality rate in the NT—which in 1958 was 138 per 1000 live births ! (Kettle 1991, Vol 2, p 325). Such were the consequences of the 'northern development' policies fostered over the course of the century by those in Canberra.

For the Aboriginal victims of these policies—the people on the pastoral properties—the issue had little to do with health services and more to do with their survival as a race. To act on this realisation, however, required more than just a concern about their future. It required the capacity to plan together, to develop a common understanding of their situation, and to stand sufficiently outside the economic lure of the pastoral stations. As they developed these capacities, the surprising thing is not that they eventually took action but that they were so patient for so long and that the pastoralists were apparently oblivious to the fact that they would eventually, but inevitably, act. From at least the mid-1940s onwards, among Aborigines

> **the question was not whether there would be a reaction, but what form this should take, and how it should be managed.**
> *(RM Berndt, quoted in Riddett p. 107)*

In developing and realising the capacity to act, a number of factors came together. Firstly, that the station workers and their families had, over the decades, maintained their links with country and retained a knowledge of traditional economic and social practice.

This meant that they were not totally dependent on station handouts—meagre though they were. Links with country were renewed through regular visits to important sites and much bush tucker knowledge was retained. In the 1960s elements of a traditional Aboriginal society and economy persisted alongside the transition society and economy of the western pastoral stations. In the turbulence of the late 1960s and 70s this cultural strength provided backbone for the various Aboriginal moves towards political self-determination which spread across the Region.

There was of course a need to overcome the isolation of the different language groups spread across the Region, to develop a common story to help make sense of the invasion. To an extent this was facilitated by the operations of the pastoral industry itself, as different groups worked together on stations and through such practices as sending Aboriginal 'boys' from one station to another for various purposes. But of course this merely reinforced the extensive communication which had always been going on between the groups:

> **One tribe used to take messages to another. The Gurindji would send word to the Bilinara, the Bilinara to the Mudbura and Ngarinman, the Mudbara to the Wardaman, and the Wardaman to the Ngaliwurru.**
> (quoted in Riddett p. 91)

And a perception of shared interest among the groups had certainly been generated by the 'one story' of violent land dispossession :

> **They reckon it's one story , every way. Ngarinmanpurru, Bilinara, Nungaliwurru, Wardaman, Warlpiri, Walman, they know. Because whitefellow never do only one place this way. Every way (they were) shooting.**

> All around Wave Hill, Warlpiri, Walman,
> Gurindji, Nyining, Jiyal, Walmayarri, Bilinara,
> Wolayijurung, Ngarinmanpurru,
> Nungaliwurru, Wardaman, all round.
> *(Anzac Munnganyi, in Rose 1991, p. 47)*

Sometimes the mixing of groups, leading to the development of a shared interest in opposing the white pastoralists, was the result of specific white-black conflicts:

> Whitefellas came after the Walbiri and they hadda run away to Wave Hill. Whitefella follow them and kill a lot of Walbiri and Gurindji. That is how Walbiri got mixed up with Gurindji people at Wave Hill.
> *(Lupgna Giari quoted in Hardy, p. 143)*

Increasingly in the postwar period, labour relations across the region were characterised by significant unrest. The views of the Director of the Native Affairs Branch draw attention to the growing frustration of the pastoralists:

> We cannot force any native to remain in any particular employment, but that is what the Northern Territory Pastoral Lessee's Association would like us to do.
> *(quoted in Riddett, p. 304)*

All the time the pressure was building, building. All the time Aboriginal people were waiting, watching: 'looking out'. And when they finally acted, they expressed the frustration of generations. The big race meetings at Negri (on Nicholson Station) and at Wyndham provided opportunities where they could compare notes.

In 1966, we went on strike from the White man. What made us do that ? They never gave us enough food and that kind of thing, and no money. They treated us like dogs, the older people, my fathers and my mother's brothers. We younger ones got angry about that. We younger ones made this (strike). The Whites used to come, but they were cheating. (They said) 'All that houses, money, you Aboriginals will get them level with the Whites.' As for that, (we got) nothing just the same. Lies they used to tell us all the time, lies. Then Ted Evans, Greenfield, who's that other white man ? It was those welfare men who used to come, sort of Patrol Officers. (They made) promise to the Aboriginals 'next year we'll improve your conditions and help you.' Then (we were) looking out, but nothing (turned up). Then we Aboriginals ourselves had a talk. (We said) 'we're making big money for the whites, but we get nothing. We must go away and leave the Whites.' Then we stayed at work, and said 'we'll watch out, next year (something might happen)'. Then we watched out, but no, still the same way. We said 'I don't think we'll get anything. We must leave them.' Then (we said) 'we'll go west to the races and see if they give us big money when we get back.' We went west for the races, and came back. We watched the white man: 'where is it, where is it, where is it ? but there was nothing. Next year we started camp again. (We said): 'no more lies, everybody on all the camps, we must all leave them right now this time all together. We must go away down to the river carrying all the children and whatever else under our arms.' West to the races (again), we had the races in the west. 'When we get back we'll leave right away' (we said). Yes (when we went for our pay, we said) 'What happened to that big pay, what happened—this one is the same again.' 'Let them stay, sorry we're finished, we had a promise seven years ago but you didn't try to do anything for us. Me and all of us we're going away, children, women and dogs (too).' With our swags on our shoulders (we went) from up there (Wave Hill Station) on this road all the way. By the river downstream from the police station we made camp, we camped two nights then an aeroplane came up with a big mob of White men, the owner Peter Morris, Cecil Watts and Tom Fisher. 'We have our heads full with you (we said). You told us lies when we were young fellows, now we have white hairs. We will not go back, not for anything.' What about if we put up your wages, and shoot two killers for you today?' (the White men said). Whatever happens,

whoever tells us to go back, we won't listen.'
(Janama, quoted in Riddett, pp. 311-312)

And so a movement started. The story of the Gurindji strike has been told elsewhere in detail—for example, in Hardy 1976—and so will not be repeated here. But some fundamental points should be emphasised as particularly relevant to the story of the Katherine West Health Board:

- The complete lack of <u>preconditions</u> necessary for good health—food, shelter etc—meant that those sporadic attempts by well-meaning nurses and doctors never had a chance of developing enough momentum to improve health in a fundamental way. Then, as now, Western medical knowledge was not an appropriate means by which to address the denuded land, vanished animal life, alienated waterholes and cultural subjugation.

- The movement towards just conditions for Aboriginal pastoral workers was not only about money. Transforming quickly into a movement for Aboriginal land rights, it was aimed at getting respect and a say for Aboriginal people in their own future.

- The fact that the movement took such a long time to build up momentum, to eventually explode in 1966, indicates the extraordinary lengths to which Aboriginal people went in order to be sure they were doing the right thing. That movement may have been a long time coming, but as the Gurindji themselves put it:

    we have never ceased to say among ourselves that Vestey's should go away and leave us to our land.
    (quoted in Riddett, p335, emphasis added)

The Gurindji walkoff set an example which was rapidly followed across the Region. In 1972 Aboriginal people from Victoria River Downs, Pigeon Hole, Moolooloo, Mt Sandford and, a little later, Humbert River, also walked off to settle at Daguragu. In 1973, many of the Victoria River Downs and Humbert River people moved from Daguragu to establish another settlement at a place they called Yarralin. Also in 1973, another group set up a camp at Bulla and commenced negotiations with Auvergne Station for their own block of land. That same year Kildurk Station was handed over to the Aboriginal people living there.

These years constituted a genuine watershed in the lives of Aboriginal people right across the Region. Out of decades of fear and desperation came initiative and hope. Suddenly Aborigines were the ones with the power, and white pastoralists had to come to terms with this or do without labour. And obtaining labour involved more than just offering money—respect had also to be on offer :

> **The point I am making is that Aborigines in this area ... will invariably work for a person who they believe has some regard and feeling for them, even if he is not able pay high wages and provide good accommodation, rather than for someone who pays very well and provides excellent accommodation but who obviously regards them as less than human—and they are not unperceptive in this respect.**
> *(Doolan 1977, p. 108-109)*

And there was the occasional pastoralist who did show "regard and feeling" for Aboriginal people—Reg Durack of Aminbidji Station, for example, is still talked about today for his kindness. But pastoralists like Reg were the exception, not the rule.

More than improved wages and conditions, Vincent Lingiari and the other leaders now planned for self-sufficient Aboriginal communities, where they would determine their own lives, free from white overseers and foreign cattle barons. The possibilities for Aboriginal-owned and operated cattle stations were talked about over nightly campfires. In setting up their new communities around this period, Aboriginal people built their own houses, dug their own latrines and constructed their own fences, demonstrating their acceptance of the point that fighting for rights and taking responsibility for their own future were two sides of the same coin.

As time has passed since those years of the walk-offs, there have been continual setbacks. Despite the referendum in 1967 which, among other things, declared that the Australian Government had the power to pass legislation for the benefit of Aboriginal people, the NT Government has never ceased its efforts to deny the residents of such communities as Daguragu, Yarralin and Pigeon Hole their basic citizenship rights. After initially refusing to provide any housing or other assistance to the people camped at Daguragu —instead spending millions on new housing and facilities at nearby Wave Hill settlement—over the years the NT Government has been reluctantly forced to accept the fact that Daguragu cannot be completely ignored. But any progress made in the region in terms of Aboriginal rights has really been through Commonwealth Government legislation, in particular the *Aboriginal Land Rights (NT) Act 1976* (which allows for inalienable Aboriginal ownership of large portions of land in the NT).

Today, Daguragu people have title to their land through this Act— but still live in substandard tin shacks and have few services. At such locations as Yarralin and Pigeon Hole, the NT Government over the years has consistently undermined all attempts to establish meaningful land rights—and consequently an economic base—for Aboriginal people whose parents provided lifetimes of servitude to the pastoral empires. Long and painful struggles to have Aboriginal living areas 'excised' from pastoral empires resulted in pathetically inadequate solutions.

At Bulla, only in 1979 was a tiny 'excision' finally granted, 6 years after Aboriginal people settled there and commenced negotiations. And at Yarralin,

> **twelve years of strikes and negotiations had produced one title under which people control an area of land which is smaller than the 240 square kilometres they had been originally promised. Hooker Company relinquished about 4% of its land ; the Yarralin mob got title to about 1.2% and the Northern Territory Government got title to about 2.8%.**
> *(Rose 1991, p. 243)*

Electricity and a reliable water supply were deliberately withheld by from Yarralin until 1985, when title to the 'excision' was handed over. One astute observer of Yarralin life summed up the situation in the late 1980s, commenting that

> **people's expectations have been flattened against a wall of circumscribed opportunities and continuing inequalities. Optimistic plans for independence have been swamped in a pervasive dependence at least equal to what was experienced before. Servitude to others had been replaced with a lassitude that is difficult to comprehend unless one has experienced it. The small blocks of land, such as the proposed Lingara block, which the**

> **Northern Territory government offers as a gesture to 'land rights', trivialise people, culture and ideas.**
> *(Rose 2000, p. 39/40)*

This, too, is part of the legacy confronting the Katherine West Health Board.

The history is somewhat brighter at other locations. At places like Amanbidji (or Kildurk/Mialuni) in the west and Lajamanu in the south, Aboriginal people finally achieved inalienable freehold title under the Land Rights Act. Despite periodic attempts by the NT Government to get the Commonwealth to water down this legislation, so far this has not happened to any great extent. Mining brought some economic benefit to the people at Lajamanu, but otherwise throughout the Region the problem has been the same: how to establish and maintain processes of genuine community development in the absence of a strong economic base and in situations where traditional life has been systematically destroyed over many decades of murder and deprivation. A key point so relevant to today's Katherine West Health Board and the issues it has to face is that in many places, social institutions have to be rebuilt from the ground up. Many people are strong and willing ; others remain traumatised from history.

And in this picture, what of health services ? Prior to the 1970s, sporadic medical surveys constituted virtually the only available services for the western cattle stations, although some of the large stations – notably Victoria River Downs and Wave Hill—employed a registered nurse. Administratively, control was divided between the Welfare Branch and the Department of Health, inhibiting the development of rational policy. With the election of a Commonwealth Labor Government in 1972, there were many new health centres established along with other huge changes, including the dismantling of the Welfare Branch. Throughout the NT, Aboriginal people living on the missions and cattle stations then became self-governing 'communities', often with their own councils. Small health clinics in these communities were progressively established, though often in situations where 'health' was seen as limited to what went on in the clinic, with the hugely inadequate preconditions for health which existed outside the clinics left unaddressed. In the Victoria River region, at Bulla and Mialuni (Amanbidji) people who were later to become Health Board members—Jack Little and Roy Harrington—were involved in a Hygiene Worker program, but battled to make progress in a situation where basic facilities were so poor.

Certainly, stretching through the 1970s, 80s and most of the 90s there was almost no effective community input into or control of the clinics. Consultation by the NT Department of Health with Aboriginal communities throughout the Katherine Region occurred only as crises arose. Aboriginal people still did not 'own' their health.

Ideas for a Health Board

The Big Picture

In the years preceding the Katherine West Health Board experiment, the notion of Aboriginal community control of health services had been slowly gaining momentum in the Northern Territory. The Central Australian Aboriginal Congress in Alice Springs, established to provide a health service operating directly under Aboriginal control and with a political agenda often in direct opposition to that of governments, broke new ground. The movement towards community control of health services, although opposed by the Northern Territory Government for many years, gradually gained acceptance as the lack of progress in dealing with Aboriginal health problems became increasingly apparent to mainstream service providers.

In Katherine, the Wurli Wurlinjang Aboriginal Health Service, governed by an elected Aboriginal Board, was set up to service Aboriginal people living in town. But in the remote communities outside of Katherine, small and generally under-funded community clinics run by the NT Government remained the only health service available. In these clinics, embattled nurses and a few brave Aboriginal Health Workers did their best to 'hold the line' against 'third world' levels of disease and grossly inadequate public and private health facilities.

In tracing the ideas which eventually led to the Katherine West Coordinated Care Trial, the remarkable thing is the convergence of a number initiatives from various sources.

At a national level, there was increasing political awareness of, and massive pressure to do something about, the appalling state of Aboriginal health. The reasons behind the lack of progress following the first National Aboriginal Health Strategy (dated 1989) had been made apparent when the Final Report of the Royal Commission Into Aboriginal Deaths In Custody specifically criticised the grossly inadequate level of funding devoted to the Strategy, and a specialist high-level committee concluded in 1994 that, while the Strategy itself may have been conceptually sound, there had never in fact been a serious attempt to implement it. The inability of ATSIC to deliver health services, illustrated by the unreliable nature of funding provided by ATSIC to Aboriginal health services was being severely criticised by the health services themselves.

The recently-appointed Aboriginal and Torres Strait Islander Social Justice Commissioner (Mick Dodson) was castigating Government inaction, and in such international forums as the United Nations Aboriginal delegates including Pat Dodson, Mick Dodson and Lois O'Donoghue of ATSIC were pointing out that 'reconciliation' was a hollow word when many Aboriginal people were either dead or in jail long before they had reached middle age.

In this way, by the mid-1990s, probably for the first time, Aboriginal health was seriously on the national agenda and the inadequacy of existing means of delivering health services had become a political issue. Among the changes being pressed for was recognition of the inadequacy of the Medical Benefits Scheme for addressing the woeful status of Aboriginal health ; an increased role for community-controlled organisations ; and the establishment of a specialised agency for Aboriginal health within the Commonwealth Department of Health.

Up in Darwin, in late 1995, Territory Health Services (THS) had been considering how to respond to a request by the Commonwealth Minister for Health, Carmen Lawrence, for expressions of interest in the idea of 'coordinated care' programs. Such expressions of interest were required for an upcoming meeting of the Council of Australian Governments (COAG), though at that time they were seen as 'mainstream' programs—that is, involving primarily non-Aboriginal populations. In THS, one or two key individuals spotted the possibility that a 'coordinated care' proposal could provide answers to some of their core problems:

> **The coordinated care trials were basically a framework that put together lots of ideas that were *already* being talked about. People were trying to look at ways of implementing ideas such as care planning, proper access to Commonwealth funding and models of community control.**
> *(Andrew Bell, THS)*

THS eventually came up with proposals for two coordinated care trials, one for the Tiwi Islands and one for the Katherine region, which were subsequently taken to the COAG meeting by the NT Government in early 1996. At this stage the 'Katherine proposal' was for the entire Katherine region involving both eastern and western sides of the NT, an area double the size of the eventual Katherine West region. The COAG meeting approved the initial expressions of interest, and THS officers Andrew Bell and Joe Wright set about writing the full proposal over the Wet Season of 1995/96. In some ways they could not anticipate how things would turn out:

> **We envisaged that the first role of the health board would be to continue purchasing existing services and decide how the money was spent. We believed that a model of community-controlled service provision might evolve from it, although we thought it possible that the health board may be the funder of a series of Aboriginal medical services. But what evolved out of it under the direction of the health board was that the**

> health board saw itself as the primary
> provider. The idea of a regional health board
> as a regional provider was not inherent in
> the original proposal—the original proposal
> just created an environment which allowed
> that.
>
> *(Andrew Bell, THS)*

The proposal received strong endorsement from within the Executive of THS, but only a lukewarm response at the level of (Katherine) District Management.

Many Players, Many Arguments

Meanwhile, back in hot and dusty Katherine, other people had been thinking along similar lines. Sitting sweating in her 'silver bullet'* office in 1995, Marion Scrymgour, then Director of the Wurli Wurlinjang Aboriginal Health Service, had been doodling with the idea of a regional body such as Wurli Wurlinjang receiving pooled funds and acting as a hub for the delivery of services through the remote region surrounding Katherine. Wurli Wurlinjang's then Medical Officer grabbed Marion's attention, saying "You need to talk to Andrew Bell in THS. Andrew's developing a paper based on these talks we've been having about pooling and having a hub in Katherine delivering services out."

And so began a process of talking, comparing and negotiating between many different players, the outcome of which no-one could predict. The process kicked off in late 1995 and early 1996. There were separate meetings between Andrew Bell of THS and

---

* 'silver bullets'—now icons of NT history—were caravans used by the NT Government to provide emergency housing and office space in remote communities when no other option was available.

the ATSIC Regional Council, and then between Andrew and Marion Scrymgour from Wurli Wurlinjang. At these meetings the proposals were presented.

Importantly, the Commonwealth Government had first endorsed the proposal for the Tiwi and Katherine Trials only on the basis of the pooling of *existing* funding, initially refusing to 'cash out' the MBS and PBS entitlements for the two Aboriginal Trials in the NT. This was despite the fact that the MBS and PBS schemes were cashed out for the mainstream trials elsewhere and despite reliable research which showed that Aboriginal people were not able to access the MBS and PBS schemes to anything like the extent which non-Aboriginal people were (Deeble 1998). THS was not prepared to accept the Commonwealth's position on this and fought against it. In an interesting comment on government processes, the eventual Commonwealth decision was made by beancounters rather than by anyone with knowledge of health or Aboriginal people:

> **We argy bargied right from the start over acknowledgement from the Commonwealth of the lack of access to Medicare and therefore it would be unfair if the existing access was enshrined in the coordinated care trial. Eventually the Department of Finance agreed, around the end of 1996, that there would be a one-times Medicare and a one-times PBS national utilisation rates 'cashout' in recognition of poor access. That was really critical because I don't think the coordinated care trials would have happened at all in the NT without that.**
> (Jenny Cleary, THS)

To add another complication to the mix, the Commonwealth Government had recently taken responsibility for funding of community-controlled Aboriginal health services from ATSIC and given it to the newly-created Office for Aboriginal and Torres Strait Islander Health (OATSIH) in the Commonwealth Department of Health. Not long after this, Marion Scrymgour left Wurli Wurlinjang to help set up the OATSIH in Darwin. Almost immediately she was drawn into the Trial proposal:

> **When I got back from one of the field trips, lo and behold what was sitting there was two proposals. One was for Tiwi and the other was for the Katherine region, from Central Office—for me to have a look at and assess whether these were going to be viable and feasible to set up. And Health Boards—to look at the costing and development of such Boards.**
> *(Marion Scrymgour)*

While all this had been happening, Andrew Bell of THS had been working the Trial proposal through the ATSIC Regional Council based in Katherine. The Regional Council accordingly wrote to all its member communities asking them to recommend models and members for the proposed interim health board, and in reply received many nominations from communities on the western side of the region but very few from the eastern side.

At that stage the THS people involved strongly believed that the Trial should cover the entire ATSIC region, both east and west sides, stating that it would have "little benefit" if confined only to one side of the region.

It was a crucial moment, and Canberra's person on the spot was Marion Scrymgour—now at OATSIH in Darwin—who could see that a Coordinated Care Trial covering the entire ATSIC region, both east and west sides, was impractical. It seems that for Marion at the time, the deciding factor was the obvious enthusiasm of local community people: "there was still something" which could not be ignored:

> The Commonwealth—OATSIH in Canberra—were getting a bit nervous and thinking maybe we'd be better off killing this—maybe it's just a means by which Territory Health are going to set up this token board as a means of laundering Commonwealth money through to the NT. But—while I was against it—there was still 'something' ... Talking to Helen Morris, who was a senior Aboriginal Health Worker out at Kalkarindji, and to people like Billy Campbell, who was also at the table, and Raymond Rose representing Lajamanu—they were people who were saying "But we've got to change our health. We're committed to changing health services for our people". And I was saying "Yeah but you can't do it over the whole of Katherine region." There was a meeting at which we pulled out a map quickly and did a line down it and we thought "Shit, we've cut this into three subregions." We put it to Andrew and the other THS mob "You people need to find out where the culture and affiliation in terms of language and ceremony, is the strongest—

> **in here or here or here. That's where you need to base your Trial because only then is it going to work, if you've got that strong affiliation between all those different language groups."**
> *(Marion Scrymgour)*

So the THS people then went back to the ATSIC Regional Council and discussed the proposal for a Trial covering only communities on the west side rather than the whole region. The Council was supportive of the idea and from there developed a three-day workshop to detail a proposal.

And that's how the Katherine Coordinated Care Trial became the Katherine West Coordinated Care Trial.

Meanwhile, another obstacle was surfacing, as it emerged that the body representing all Aboriginal community-controlled health services in the NT—the Aboriginal Medical Services Alliance Northern Territory, or AMSANT—had been lobbying the new Commonwealth Minister for Health, Michael Wooldridge, to stop the Katherine and Tiwi Trials going ahead. In a paper sent to Minister Wooldridge prior to final approval by the Commonwealth of the Katherine West Trial, AMSANT alleged the Trials breached key recommendations of the Royal Commission Into Aboriginal Deaths In Custody. AMSANT's objections focussed particularly on the alleged lack of involvement of Wurli Wurlinjang Aboriginal Health Service in the Trial, which it said would result in duplication and financial faults in the funding model, and on the risk of Commonwealth money being absorbed to subsidise costs which should otherwise be met by Territory Health Services.

Marion took the issue head-on, directly negotiating with Wes Miller of Wurli Wurlinjang, then also Executive Secretary of

AMSANT, and secured an agreement with Wurli Wurlinjang that the Trial should proceed, largely on the basis that 'we'll see what happens'. The impact of Marion's influence on the Trial proposal is apparent in Wurli Wurlinjang's letter of (conditional) support to OATSIH in Canberra:

> **Wurli Wurlinjang supports in principle the conduct of the Development Phase of the Trial in the hope that our concerns ... are considered during this Phase. The recent downsizing of the Trial area by more than 50% has influenced us in giving this support....**
>
> **We note with approval the recent addition of Marion Scrymgour to the Trial.... We are confident of her ability to conduct sensitive and thorough community consultations...**

Fortunately, the personal touch also worked with the other key players in AMSANT:

> **I met with Pat (Anderson) and said to her 'Come on Pat, you know what I'm like, I'm not going to do anything that's going to prop up THS. My whole focus and my wanting to have this work is for the communities, not for Territory Health.' And Pat said 'Alright, we'll stand back'—which they did.**
> *(Marion Scrymgour)*

The eventual written recommendation from OATSIH to the Secretary of the Commonwealth Department of Health reflected this situation, saying:

> **AMSANT has raised some issues which the Department acknowledges and will respond to. However, there are opportunities in the development phase to sort through these matters, and therefore no cause to abandon the Katherine Trial.**

It should be emphasised that the agreement between Wes Miller and Marion was politically risky for both of them. Although things did eventually 'work out', it is just another instance of the many occasions when the Katherine West Trial could have fallen over before it had even begun.

In the end, Wurli Wurlinjang gave assistance by acting as interim fundholder and providing temporary office space for the new Katherine West Trial.

The differing perspectives held and tactics employed by all the various players within these organisations came close to exploding on more than one occasion. Without the ability of all stakeholders to get together and compromise, and without a committed person with good political judgement in the middle, the chances of getting such a radical initiative off the ground would have been slim.

> **To try to keep your finger on where everything was happening was an impossible task but one that we did achieve in the end... The stresses of in terms of worrying**

> and making sure that I had all my bases covered in terms of Wurli and AMSANT, Territory Health, the Commonwealth and the community—there were four major players in this and I had to make sure that I sat squarely in the middle to pull it all together.
> *(Marion Scrymgour)*

In moving the Trial past AMSANT's objections Marion had also committed herself to a much greater personal responsibility to ensuring that it worked:

> Although disputed by THS, as the Trial went on there turned out to be a lot of truth in what AMSANT had been saying. But rather than having those discussions with the Aboriginal people on the ground, AMSANT went directly to government bureaucrats…Their case would have held more water and been a lot stronger if AMSANT as the peak political body had gone directly to the people in the community and even the health centre staff and said "Have you been consulted in this ?" AMSANT would have found that hardly anyone had been consulted. That was the task. Once Territory Health had agreed to Katherine West, they found that there was no-one within the department that had the skills or expertise to then go and do the consultations, to go and sell that proposal to the communities.
> *(Marion Scrymgour)*

Organising in the Communities

Then began a lengthy period of direct consultation which, in developing a genuine commitment which transcended conventional bureaucratic structures, turned out to be a crucial process:

> So I convinced OATSIH to let me go out into the Katherine region just to try and ascertain what level of support there was without raising any expectations, but saying to people 'What if you had a chance to do this, would you do it ?' This was just me walking around and talking to people.
>
> A lot of them said 'Yeah, sounds good—but is it going to change?' But I was amazed at the fears that there were from Aboriginal people. The selling point wasn't so much the money, it was the control. Remember these people are on the receiving end of the history where they've had no control, they've been suppressed for years. Some of them did say to me 'We've heard governments say things before, we've heard…' And that's where Jack Little drew that picture which showed the strong line which went from Aboriginal people to their communities in terms of what they say and their oral history. What's been handed down through the generations has always been the same thing and it's strong. But in terms of governments,

> governments change all the time, so in Jack's picture that was a broken line.
>
> Jack was saying 'Oh yeah, you know my girl, you doing good job but these government mob, they're not going to give up easily you know, they're not going to give us the control straight away, they'll only give us little bit and we gonna have to fight all the time.'
>
> And I kept saying to him 'No, no, no, we'll make sure.' And that's where I was naive, in thinking this was going to be transferred immediately to the board. But that old bloke was quite adamant, saying 'No, no, we're going to have to prove every time we do something, we're gonna be out to prove ourselves.'
>
> And he was right, old Jack, you know.
> *(Marion Scrymgour)*

Jack has himself described his awareness of history, and his early doubts:

> When the government people come they promise one thing. When they go home, something that's very important that the community people been ask for, well nothing happen.
> *(Jack Little, KWHB Board member)*

The importance of this should not be underestimated—it was (and is) a widespread view in the region, gained from hard experience and not easily negated. Speaking of one prominent man from Yarralin, Debbie Rose summed up the experience of most Aboriginal people who had been dealing with whitefella bureacuracies:

> **When Hobbles (Danayarri) told me that he had decided to stop attending meetings with European bureaucrats, he said that for years he had 'sweetened' himself up just like tea, trying to make himself and others understood, and 'nothing been come back. Just nothing.'**
> *(Rose 2000, p.195)*

Jack, however, eventually decided to give it a go :

> **We focussing and think what Aboriginal people need—get more knowledge and understanding and make things happen. That's the reason why... Like maybe some white bloke don't believe us very much sometime, but too long we been under control by white people, and this is our first opportunity to, you know, 'come on, get up and help ourselves.'**

> **When I first heard about it, I wasn't too sure whether the health board was going to be working but anyway I went in and had a go ... But I didn't think it's happening now, something like Aboriginal control....**

> **The health board been start up and it's sort of to Aboriginal people in the community. Just like Daguragu strike and things like that, they had a bit of power too and someone been helping them to get to that state. And now, this Katherine West been putting something in our heart to make our own strike to build that up.**
> (Jack Little, KWHB Board member)

The dynamics of political organising at community level were fundamental to the eventual functioning of the Board and to maintaining *genuine* community support. Hence it is of value to go into the details of how this was done. One tactic in the communities was to seek as wide a level of representation as possible, including those from outside the usual power hierarchy and both young and old:

> **I went to the leaders and I said to them 'I need to consult with everybody'. Because I was leading up to actually electing representatives from those communities, and I didn't want just the main leaders. To get a board where people were just focussed on health, and not on ATSIC, not on the council, not on the store committee—it was important to try and get fresh blood and people who would see health as their main priority.**
>
> **I was having to manoeuvre around and be very sensitive in the consultation with leaders who for a long time manipulated certain systems for their gain and I didn't want that, not with the health board. I**

thought 'If this is going to work it's got to come from people who are not going to manipulate it for their own cause, but rather be there because they're committed to change to health and for the good of their community.'

While also wanting the leaders' support, I set about meticulously going through all the Government requirements. It was good at that time because Pauline Hansen was coming out with 'Aboriginals abuse everything and money gets stolen.' And so I utilised what she was saying as a means of, you know: 'If we're gonna make this work, we've got to do it properly otherwise this is going to be another thing for that red-headed woman to pick up and say 'look at this, you give blackfellas this money and control and look what happens'. '

A lot of the young men and young women stood back because they felt this is all going to be the older people and certain power brokers in the community are going to dominate things. It was a big shock to their system when I'd go and say 'look I think you should be a part of this.' It was amazing going to all the clinics—even though this Trial was ready to get going, not one nurse in the clinics had been consulted.
(Marion Scrymgour)

Another important lesson for community organising was the need to identify key individuals who had particularly strong visions of what needed to be done, and enlist their support. Most of the time these were Helen Morris and Jack Little.

> **Jack and Helen were the best two mentors that anyone could have ever had. I grabbed old Jack because I was captivated by that old man's vision and where he kept saying 'Yeah yeah we're going to fight for this and it's got to be done this way.' That's where I've always felt privileged, that I was able to work through those barriers of cultural acceptance with men, and a lot of that was helped by old Jack.**
>
> **Because I'm not from that region, I went into that thinking I don't know anything and allowed these two—Helen and Jack—to lead me. I was passing my skills and information to them two and it was them two that was driving the process.**
>
> **All the consultations involved painting a picture about the old way, talking about how the old way of health and how health services were delivered, and if the Trial went ahead the new way, and how things would happen. 'If you had a chance to fix your health and the health of your community, what would you do? And you tell me how, if we set up this organisation what would we need to do. How would we need to change**

> it?' And that's where community control came in. It was amazing how any concerns and complaints came out in these consultations. The biggest thing they wanted to change was the gender balance in the clinics. A lot of men were saying we don't go into the clinics because there's all females.
>
> We would have sessions where I would sit down with Helen when we went and spoke to women. I'd go through the different papers with her and we'd just scribble things down. We would then go to the meetings and she would stand up and translate all of that in language. It was her driving the process. I did the same with Jack. Mostly we did it in a lot of little groups.
>
> I used to keep the local councils informed of what was happening, but it was not going to the council or using the council, it was going directly to the community to talk with the community.
> *(Marion Scrymgour)*

Jack described his motivation for this work:

> We didn't get paid for it. We been passing on something that they never heard before and we board members, we thought about it we are doing something not for the Katherine West (but) for the people in the communities. And that's the reason why.

> **We wanted to run as quickly as we can to build up the idea to community people so they can understand really.**
> *(Jack Little, KWHB Board member)*

And Helen was motivated by the possibility of *real* change, at last :

> **All the local people came out and started listening to what's going to be happening, and it was a really exciting thing—we're going to start our own board ... But we took it slowly, bits and pieces... Because we was looking forward, it was really exciting and we finally got it through !**
> *(Helen Morris, KWHB Board member)*

To complete the consultation process, Marion moved over from OATSIH to be employed by THS. This time spent consulting turned out to be contentious from the point of view of the Commonwealth Government, but it turned out to be essential in order to develop genuine community understanding of the momentous changes about to take place:

> **It took a long time, the whole consultation phase was about eight months and I'd say six of those eight months the communities held coordinated care at a distance.**
> *(Marion Scrymgour)*

This view of Marion received support from some within THS :

> **I think the Commonwealth just *entirely* underestimated how long it takes for any new initiative to be explained and thought**

> through and argy bargied and re-explained and so on, and for leaders to emerge from communities around the specific issues that you're dealing with and all those community development processes. Just completely underestimated them. I'm talking about Canberra.
>
> *(Jenny Cleary, THS)*

Following this period, all communities were invited in May 1997 to send representatives to a meeting in Katherine, and in this way the Interim Board was formed—though yet to be incorporated.

The End of the Beginning

Throughout all this process the Commonwealth had been delaying final approval—attached to funding—for the Trial to actually proceed. The Tiwi Islands Trial had already been approved and funded. But the Katherine West Trial was a different story, partly because of delays caused by indecision about the size of the region to be covered and partly because of the problems caused by AMSANT's lack of support—AMSANT had developed a close and influential relationship with Minister Wooldridge's personal staff. And if it to was to go ahead the Commonwealth insisted that everything had to be up and running on the 1st September.

But it was already July—and time for answers. Marion took some members of the Interim Board members—Helen Morris, Raymond Rose, Joseph Cox, Noreen Raven and Billy Campbell—to Canberra, and pleaded with the Commonwealth Government for a final decision to fund the Development Phase, and to put back the commencement date. Helen's letter requesting a meeting made the point that

> **We know that there has been a lot of scepticism and wariness about the community managing health funds and whether we are able to cope with this. To date, not one of those people have attempted to come and sit down with us ... We know it will be hard, and there will be mistakes along he way, but we should be given the opportunity to make them and how to overcome these problems for ourselves.**
>
> *(Letter Helen Morris, KWHB, to Minister Wooldridge)*

This face to face articulation by Aboriginal people of their hopes and concerns directly to Canberra was timed perfectly and was able to overcome immense political barriers. Because of this human approach, Minister Wooldridge was prepared to overrule his personal staff on the issue:

> **Robert Griew (of OATSIH in Canberra) was quite honest with us and said 'Look, Wooldridge doesn't hold much hope for Katherine West. AMSANT's position (opposing the Trial) is quite strong.'**
>
> **We came back to Darwin, those guys went back to their communities and I'd gone into THS and was sitting there, and Robert Griew rang and he said 'Are you sitting down?' And I said 'Yes, what for?' And he says 'You've got the Trial'.**
>
> **I remember sitting there and I felt like crying. It was 'Okay, now I've got it, what am**

I going to do?' At the same time I felt really elated that against all odds I'd managed to get this up. I was determined—and one thing that I'd have is a very stubborn streak, and if I get a bee in my bonnet, I'll stubbornly pursue that.
(Marion Scrymgour)

Early Days for the Board

Paper and Problems

Shortly after advising Marion that she'd 'got the Trial', OATSIH in Canberra agreed to move the starting date of the Development Phase back, allowing some breathing space, but insisted that the Live Phase must start in July 1998.

It seems that almost everyone involved—and especially those OATSIH people situated in the remote city of Canberra—hugely underestimated the amount of work that had yet to be done. To illustrate this point, a Schedule attached to the Legal Agreement governing the Development Phase of the Trial listed the following 'Key Deliverables':

- A draft funding model

- Final proposal of funding model

- Final proposal of cost modelling

- 30% of care plans drafted

- Progress report regarding curriculum development

- Care plans completed

- Care Coordinators' curriculum completed

- 30% of required number of Care Coordinators trained

- Finalised recruitment procedures for Care Coordinators

- Draft methodology for data collection for local and national evaluation

- Final methodology for data collection and management

- Draft recruitment procedures for trial communities and individuals

- Finalisation of recruitment of communities and individuals into trial

- Draft of service delivery phase budget

- Finalised service delivery phase budget

- Draft of Katherine West Health Board's training needs analysis

- Training of Katherine West health Board underway

Within each of these broad 'deliverables' lay numerous subtasks, each daunting on its own. Just to consider the issue of recruitment of individuals into the Trial, for example, the Health Insurance Commission required a signed and witnessed consent form from each individual in a situation where the 'consentors' were scattered across a huge region, had little or no standard English, had never heard of the Health Insurance Commission or Medicare, and frequently had more than one name.

And if Aboriginal community control was to really mean something, most of the things on this whitefella agenda had to be managed by a small group of people with limited literacy and experience of such things. And on top of this there was the added responsibility on Board members of developing and maintaining support for the Trial in the communities. It was an unprecedented test of commitment.

> Raymond Rose, Helen Morris, Jack Little, Joseph Cox and Noreen Raven. They would come in and we all used to sit down—it was like my little working group. Every week they was coming in and that went on for at least six months. They weren't getting paid—THS was covering their accommodation and incidental allowances for food and stuff—and that's where Territory Health to their credit had picked up a lot of other funding and expenses that the Commonwealth wouldn't pick up. But these community people were removed from their families for weeks on end.
>
> And they weren't only coming into meetings in Katherine. I was having to bring them into Darwin for all these rounds of meetings with THS people. And even though you'd try to get them to break down that information (about coordinated care) for our mob, even though they were Health Workers, it was still complex.
>
> We finally opened our office in Katherine, then the Australia Day floods happened in January 98—and we lost everything. But still the Commonwealth insisted that the Live Phase must commence on July 98.
> *(Marion Scrymgour)*

As it turned out, not all the tasks listed to be completed before July 1998 were actually completed by that date and many were carried over into the Live Phase period of the Trial itself. Undoubtedly this was largely due to sheer scope of the projects, although it should be noted that KWHB expressed its view at the time that THS was not —even at this early stage—meeting its commitment regarding progress towards computerisation in its community health centres and training of staff in care coordination.

Of course at the same time the Board members and Marion were negotiating with both Governments, not always amicably. Eventually crunch time came when Marion was told by the Commonwealth that, when working with the Board, she had a duty of care to the Commonwealth regarding confidential government information. On the spot she resigned.

The Board members then told the Governments they wanted Marion to continue working with them and rather than advertise the Administrator's (later changed to Director's) position, they offered the job to her.

And so Marion became the first Director of the Katherine West Health Board. From the perspective of the Board members, the offer was made because they had come to appreciate her personal commitment :

> **When we saw Marion we didn't look at her colour, we look at her.**
> *(Jack Little, KWHB Board member)*

But the contract between the Board and Marion was more than just a salary in return for work. Most importantly, it involved a contract for honesty and commitment which was binding on both sides:

> **It's being honest to those members and saying to them 'Don't waste my time. If I'm going to take this on, I want 100 per cent**

commitment.' And that needs to be said to them. If they want it they will take it. But it's got to be done in an open honest way to them.
(Marion Scrymgour)

Whitefellas on the Board?

Early on the Board had to deal with the fact that not all people residing in the Katherine West Region were Aborigines. Many cattle stations were operated by non-Aboriginal pastoralists, and the town of Timber Creek had a mixed Aboriginal and non-Aboriginal population. An important issue to be resolved early on was the role of non-Aboriginal people in the proposed Trial.

As far as actual health services was concerned, the main Aboriginal people involved set out from the start to ensure inclusive coverage —but not control.

> **I took Jack Little, Helen Morris and Joseph Cox to a meeting with the Cattlemen's Association, and Jack was very keen to point out to them that while this Trial was targeting Aboriginal health problems, the Interim Board didn't want to isolate the non-Aboriginal people but wanted them to be part of it. But representation on the Board was always going to be an issue.**
> *(Marion Scrymgour)*

The way in which the new Board was to be incorporated was crucial in this respect. Northern Territory incorporation legislation allowed membership on the basis of residence, thereby leaving open the possibility for membership by non-Aboriginal people. In contrast, the Commonwealth's Aboriginal Councils and Associations Act allowed membership only to Aboriginal people. According to Marion, Territory Health Services had been insisting upon incorporation under NT legislation.

> **After I had sat down and analysed the whole situation I thought 'This isn't going to work—this is going to be targeting Aboriginal people's chronic and acute illnesses. So if this was going to be set up for Aboriginal people and controlled by Aboriginal people, the incorporation has to be under Commonwealth legislation.'**
> *(Marion Scrymgour)*

In that way non-Aboriginal people were excluded from the new Board. But as residents of the region they could not be ignored, and they had a powerful lobby group—the NT Cattlemen's Association—representing their interests.

> **So as a compromise we said 'Let's incorporate under Commonwealth legislation but let's make concessions in the incorporation to develop a sub-committee of the Executive that would allow non-Aboriginal people to have a platform in which to go through their issues.**
>
> **Which seemed to satisfy them, but there are still issues about which they continue to say 'why don't we have representation on the Board ?' That won't stop. But one day they'll get sick of saying it because things won't change.**
> *(Marion Scrymgour)*

So the Cattle Stations Consumer Sub-Committee was established and now provides feedback to the Board on issues of concern to pastoralists.

In another move to provide a service to the pastoralists, the Board decided to set up a travelling health service to visit all the cattle stations—this was an improvement on the level of service to these stations which had existed before the Trial, and in the long run did much to defuse opposition to the KWHB from that source.

This travelling service, operating out of a converted Toyota Landcruiser, is staffed by two registered nurses and one Aboriginal Health Worker. It provides many evening clinics and screening sessions, accessible to all people on the stations, with a large health promotion component emphasising healthy lifestyles. During 2000, this service provided over four hundred consultations. The service also runs accredited first aid training courses for station residents where possible. In late 2000 the Executive Director of the NT Cattlemen's Association wrote to the KWHB stating that

> **Those people who reside in the area covered by the service regard it as extremely successful. It fills an essential role in providing the standard of health which urban residents of Australia regard as a right. The Association is fully supportive of the Mobile Health Service, and is hopeful that it will not only continue to operate, but will do so on an expanded basis.**

Training

Community control was just meaningless jargon unless the Board members really understood what was going on. With knowledge comes power to run their own affairs. So a key issue early on was how to give the members genuine understanding and knowledge.

But in this, as in every other issue, there were obstacles. The first one was money.

> **One of the things I wrote was looking at training of those members—and the Commonwealth was never convinced that was a good thing. They kept saying we don't have funding for the training and if you want to train these members you're going to have to do it out of your existing funding. So it was playing with a inadequate budget.**
> (Marion Scrymgour)

Focusing on the areas of human resources and financial management, Marion and the members looked around to see what training was available.

> **I went to Street Ryan and Consultants, I went to NTETA, I went to LGANT, I went to ATSIC to look at all their papers in terms of what they have for training of their elected arm. Nothing was there—it had no substance —no wonder this mob can't operate effectively!**
> (Marion Scrymgour)

Eventually Marion remembered Hugh Lovesy, who had been trying unsuccessfully to get funding to do his 'Money Story' training package with communities in Central Australia. So near the end of 1997, Marion engaged Hugh's company, Pangaea Pty Ltd, to work with the Board on the issues of the roles and responsibilities of Board members, financial accountability and human resources. There was no time for Hugh to do the 'needs analysis' which would normally precede a training package—instead, everyone had to jump in together and see what happened: an 'ongoing needs analysis' was combined with the actual delivery of training.

From the very first session, the criteria by which the training was judged was that of genuine understanding, not just a nodding of heads:

> **The main performance indicator throughout all the training is whether the information discussed at the training sessions can be passed on to other Board members not present or other members not present.**
> (Draft Report, Pangaea Pty Ltd)

In developing many of the training concepts, Hugh was able to utilise the ideas put forward by some of the Board members themselves. For example, the metaphor of the Health Board as a rainwater tank, receiving money from governments and then using it for communities, was first put up by Jack as a way of explaining the need for training and for Board members to accept responsibility:

> **We have to fix the problem ourselves and not rely on other people to do it. We need to look at what is causing the problem. If we don't look after the tank and if the tank gets a hole the money will go somewhere else. We all make mistakes and we learn from our mistakes**
> (Jack Little, at workshop on 3 July 1997)

Hugh was able to develop Jack's concept of 'stopping leaks from the tank' over the coming months in his training package.

The context in which the training was required determined the nature of the training provided. And the context was that Board members saw themselves as sitting in an informational 'no mans land' between governments and communities, a situation made more difficult by the inability of governments to present information in a form which was comprehensible.

> The Executive members are particularly concerned they are sandwiched between two difficult situations. Firstly, and most importantly mass information being presented by Government Departments to the Executive and Board. The Government Departments, with a few notable exceptions, have made no special effort to make sure the material that is being presented is of a very clear nature, which could be quickly and easily understood.
>
> On the other hand the Board is very concerned that information should flow down through the Board to community members. Without community members understanding what the Trial is about and giving it their support, it is unlikely that a high level of success will be achieved in the Trial.
>
> The Administrator has, on the advice of the Board, contacted several Government Departments and asked them to make much more effort in simplifying information that's flowing into the Executive and Board. However, despite one or two exceptions, Government Departments have not made any significant response to this request.
> *(Draft Report, Pangaea Pty Ltd)*

In the way in which it was used at Katherine West, 'training' is an inadequate word. It was not simply the transfer of information or 'facts' from one head to another. Rather, it was a constant process of negotiation between different knowledges, with the outcome being a hybrid which in effect mediated between two cultures. Probably the best example of this is a diagram of two roads to health which the Board developed as a way of illustrating such mediation. The 'Two Roads' picture became the Board's signature document :

Over the years of the Trial, the cultural mediation practiced by Pangaea and the Board under the name of 'training' turned out to be invaluable. Mostly it covered 'The Money Story'—a pictorial representation of financial accounts—but also it had to deal with such concepts as the notion of 'provider-funder-purchaser' separation of roles (dealt with by people literally putting on 'different hats') and many other tricky issues.

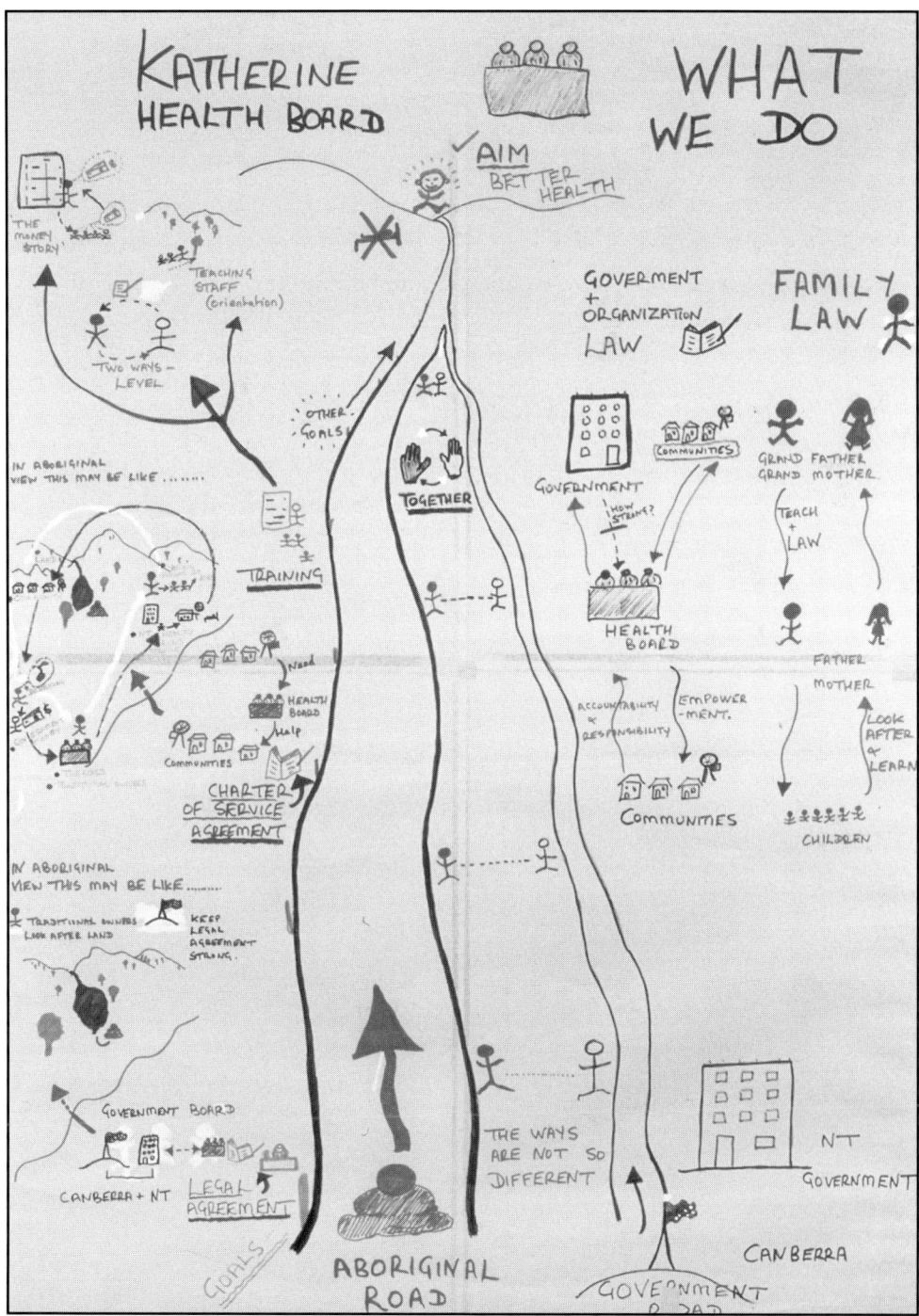

The Two-Roads Poster

A Training Case Study

The practical nature and immense value of the training provided is illustrated by a key decision the Board members had in mid-1998. The general principle at stake was a common one in Aboriginal organisations. But the way in which this decision was approached by the Board – rationally and with a full appreciation of all relevant perspectives – makes it unique. The following is taken from a report by Pangaea Pty Ltd.

Two important Board members had proposed that they be given paid positions as liaison officers and that vehicles be bought for them and a budget allocated for their use. However there was no existing budget to allow for such expenditure. If such expenditure were to occur then it would have to come out of money that was earmarked for direct expenditure on health work (MBS abd PBS funds). If Board members were to agree to this proposal then the two members would have benefited greatly but the group would have been worse off as important health programs would have had to have been cut back to pay for their salaries and vehicle costs.

The first problem that the Board members had to resolve was this: 'Is it right that these two members take part in a decision in which there is a conflict of interest ? If they were to act as Board members then they would most likely vote for the benefit of the group and support the continuation of the important health programs. If they were to act as employees (workers) of the Board then they would be most likely to vote for their own benefit which was to get themselves jobs and vehicles.'

The second problem that the Board members had to resolve was this: 'If the Board members agreed to this proposal than they would have agreed to a situation in which future conflicts of interest would be highly likely to arise. This would have acted as a precedent which would have encouraged other Board members to make the same demands. The Board could have become seriously weakened and the whole Trial could have been threatened. An important step towards Aboriginal self-management could have been stopped dead in its tracks.'

During the training session it was repeatedly pointed out that the training was to provide clear information only. The Board members were the people who were going to take the decision. The trainer used drawings and charts during the sessions. The main thrust of the training was to take concepts like empowerment, roles and conflict of interest and place them in an Aboriginal framework. This was done by (1) discussing these concepts in a family relationship and getting participants to bring forward their own comments and observations (2) discussing these concepts in a halfway house situation where Aboriginal and European frameworks interact daily at a community level (the Board members were very familiar with the pressures of reconciling the two frameworks at this level) – for instance would it be good for the families in the community if the chairman were to write out his own orders for fuel or for a new Toyota for himself ? (3) Finally the concepts were discussed in the context of the Health Board.

The Board members were very active during this training, saying it was useful and helped them. One of the two people who were in a conflict of interest situation said they appreciated the relevance of the training to their situation. The Board asked the two members to present their case in full but to be absent when the final decision was being made. The Board also decided that no staff or other people should be present when they took their decision. They made clear that if they were to have agreed to the proposals that there would have been a conflict of interest. This was the reason they refused to allocate resources for 2 extra salaries and purchase of vehicles.

The Board members faced a difficult decision. They were clear that they too faced a conflict of interest between their own roles in terms of traditional family and kinship relations to the two Board members and their roles as Board members of an organisation that is empowering a large group of Aboriginal people by increasing self-management of their own health services. However this was an unavoidable conflict of interest. They were happy that staff and trainer trusted their judgement as to what for them and their constituents was the best decision to make.

Information is Power

In planning for the Live Phase, the Board members had to first deal with the reluctance of THS to provide full and complete financial data. In principle, THS had agreed to 'pool' all the money which they would have otherwise spent on primary health care services in the Katherine West region. Only if they knew exactly how much this was would the Board members be able to take real decisions reflecting their own priorities—otherwise they ran the risk of being just a 'token Board'. AMSANT had already alleged this may happen, and Marion had put her personal reputation on the line when she had talked AMSANT into not opposing the Trial. So accurate financial information was a key requirement. Two of the issues were : would the pooled amounts include 'on-costs' and the costs of employing staff at the 'establishment' levels set by THS?

> **They'd given us a spreadsheet but there was no detail or information about how they'd reached the amounts on that spreadsheet. So it was months of banging our heads, saying to THS at meetings 'How can the Board accept this figure when we don't have the information to see how you reached them ?' They all used to sit there and say 'Trust us'. And I was saying 'How can you sit there and tell them to trust you mob ? Look at the history that these people have had with health services out there.' What we wanted was two financial years historical information so that we could see what their actual costs were, and then have a look at it**

based upon the pooled amount to see if there was any difference. THS was saying 'Our government system won't allow us to pull this information out.' So our Executive members stood up and said 'If you won't do it we're going to walk away from this.' Then the Commonwealth went into a big flap and closed the meeting down, demanding that the THS people come back with that information in two hours. And it was amazing—all these months we'd been trying to get that information and they produced it in two hours.

So for the Board members it was really good exposure for them to sit back and watch all of this. And Jack used to sit there all the time and say 'I told you. I told you'. He was the one who was always very strong in terms of the governments' big mob of bullshit.

When we took those figures away, and I got some advice and weighed things up and went back to the Board and said 'You can either walk away now and forget it, because there's huge shortfalls here in terms of what they've pooled versus what they've really spent on health services, or bite the bullet and say OK we know what THS is pooling but we can use the extra money we get from the Commonwealth, and set about trying to make this coordinated care work as our first

> priority.' So the Board had to make a decision within four weeks—in the end they agreed to bite the bullet, even though they knew the risk involved because the pool was inadequate.
>
> *(Marion Scrymgour)*

Although on the occasion described above, a Commonwealth officer had insisted that THS provide detailed cost information, in fact the Commonwealth had earlier vetoed any such requirement being in the Legal Agreement covering the Live Phase of the Trial. When negotiating the terms of this Legal Agreement, the KWHB had suggested an amendment to a clause setting out THS' responsibilities, along the following lines:

> At the request of the Health Board provide Trial services on reasonable terms and conditions and ... at no more than the cost of the services calculated by reference to the Proposal (<u>the method and figures arrived at as a result of such calculation to be agreed upon between the parties, but failing such agreement, to be determined by the National Evaluator for Aboriginal and Torres Strait Islander Trials</u>) and otherwise at a reasonable cost.

Inclusion of the underlined words in this clause had been the KWHB's suggested amendment, with the intention that there would then be a process established under the authority of the Live Phase Agreement which would involve the delivery up by THS of both historical service delivery costing data and ongoing data of the same kind.

The Commonwealth's response to this proposed amendment was to send it back to the KWHB with the annotation "Delete – not relevant". In doing this, the Commonwealth absolved THS of responsibility for efficient service provision and placed the KWHB in a position of great uncertainty for much of the Trial. The consequences of this became apparent during the Live Phase.

Into the Live Phase

Decisions and Priorities

As mentioned previously in this study, the THS people who wrote the initial Trial proposal did not envisage that the Board would necessarily want to take over direct management of the health centres (clinics) in communities. It is an indication of how keen they were to run their own affairs—to create something new—that in fact the Board members wanted to take direct control *from the beginning* of the Trial. But doubts about the scope of the funds pool meant this had to be put on hold:

> I'd convinced the Board to defer control of the management for a year or so, so that we could work through the financial side, saying 'OK once we've gone through a year, let's look at the money it's taken to run these clinics, then we can work out what percentage of Commonwealth money we're going to need to use to top up, or work with THS to give us the extra money for the shortfall.'
>
> So for the first year we'd just give THS the resources. One of the best exercises to happen was that we invited all of the THS staff from the communities to come in and meet with the Executive and asked those staff members 'You tell us. What are your needs in those clinics ? How are we going to make this work ?' And THS was quite miffed about this, but that's how we got the

> suggestion to employ an administrative person in each clinic.
> *(Marion Scrymgour)*

Much of the early period of the Live Phase was taken up with two things : observing how much it really cost to run the health centres (clinics), and debate between the Board members and senior staff about strategies to tackle the health needs in communities. From the beginning it was apparent that many Board members already had ideas about what to do. They had been quietly thinking about things right from the first consultations when they had been asked the 'what if …' questions. From such thinking as this came ideas such as employing their own GPs and placing them fulltime in communities.

A key theme which weaved its way throughout these debates was the priority to be given to funding clinical services, on the one hand, and improving health services in the communities—outside the clinical centres—on the other. The KWHB was committed under the terms of the Legal Agreement to giving first priority to providing a certain level of clinical services. Yet the Board members also had their own ideas, and did not always see things from the perspective which had applied in the past.

> **It would frustrate Michael (the KWHB's first Medical Director) and me and we'd say 'No but you need to do this' and they'd say 'Yeah, that kardiya (whitefella) way, we want to do this.' Like, they fought us tooth and nail about the clinics, because most of the Board members wanted the programs out in the community—they wanted programs to start happening out there, not in the clinics.**

> We were saying—because I suppose I had the blinkers on too—'Yeah but you can't have these programs happen unless you get the resources in the clinics'. We were always saying 'Yeah, but what about this and that?' and they'd say 'No, let's get back to this.'
>
> They then agreed to 'Ok our first thing is to resource the clinics – that's the extra admin and nursing staff ' and once we got the clinics up to it they stuck to their guns about environmental health and nutrition services outside in the community.
> (*Marion Scrymgour*)

These arguments were not only about programs but also about the roles of staff:

> Jack and Helen have always been strong about getting the Health Workers out of the clinics and into the community. They don't see the importance of the competency standards and skills that mainstream society has demanded of these Health Workers. They see their community skills and community competencies as being fundamental, not the ones they use in the clinic. That's been where the Board members have always disagreed with us.
> (*Marion Scrymgour*)

Not being aware of what was going on behind the scenes, Governments were getting increasingly edgy. From the point of view of the bureaucracies in Canberra and Darwin, the Live Phase of the Trial was only going to be 18 months long and their political masters required a positive outcome in that short time frame.

Governments and Aboriginal People: Negotiating Roles

The two Governments expressed their frustration in different ways and with different rationales—but it seems neither of them really appreciated the debates going on behind the scenes between Board members and staff over how to allocate their newly acquired funds, or the reluctance of the Board to simply hand over responsibility for all the new paperwork and procedural issues to whitefella staff. Both of these factors—characterised by an emphasis on process rather than outcome—took up a lot of the new Board's time.

Marion Scrymgour's perspective was that the KWHB had had to devote too much time and resources to the process of recruitment, on the one hand, while allowing time for communities themselves to generate proposals, on the other.

> **In hindsight, the task of recruiting individuals to the Trial ... the Board should have left this task with THS as originally planned in the beginning of the Trial's development ...**
>
> **There are some indications that the Commonwealth is uneasy about the size of the KWHB's existing MBS/PBS surplus. It is assumed that such a surplus reflects a failure of the Trial to effectively meet community health needs ... This assumption fails to acknowledge the length of time necessary**

> for participating communities to self-assess their own health priorities to their own satisfaction...
> *(Report by Marion Scrymgour to the KWCCT Monitoring Group, 20/5/99)*

From the Commonwealth's point of view, at the time Canberra was

> very concerned with the Katherine West Trial—it had been going for a year and there'd been huge amounts of money spent on travel and meetings, accommodation expenses and that but nothing had really happened. Then suddenly it just exploded with all this activity and you had the taking over of the clinics and a lot of new programs coming on board in a short time. Marion Scrymgour had argued all along that there has to be this sense of ownership, and that's eventually what happened. But to get that takes a long time—you're talking about 15, 16 months of continual meetings in the bush, in town, explaining to people what a health board does—empowering them so that they know what questions to ask, what it should be doing—because no-one knew their rights in health.
> *(Kirk Whelan, Commonwealth Dept of Health & Aged Care)*

THS' point of view was that

> we were having the Evaluation over this finite time period, and Katherine West Health Board kept focussing on political issues : the size of their funding pool, the structure of their organisation, and other things like their relationships with community councils and those sorts of things.
>
> There was a certain sense of unease around the slowness and a couple of times we got messages in meetings from board members about 'Why doesn't THS put in more this and more that?'. We felt we had to go right back to first base and say 'Well you've got the money, not us'. This was totally expectable, but it just seemed to us that people hadn't yet taken on board the fact that it was all in their power to do it.
> *(Jenny Cleary, THS)*

The Minutes of the meeting of the Trial Monitoring Group on 12 January 1999 provides an insight into the difficulties which the various parties saw in developing their roles:

> Jack Little (KWHB) said he would like to see things happen in the communities. Community people were asking questions. When is something going to happen. Government people are going out bush and saying things but nothing is happening.

Lorraine Johns (KWHB) asked when are dental and STD people going to start visiting.

Rose Rhodes (THS) said this was a good question and she would like to know when the Board intended to undertake these services...

Marion Scrymgour (KWHB) said money is now starting to be spent through MBS/PBS. She further said that at the end of the day the funding provided was not enough (and that) the Board seemed to be resourcing THS clinics. Michelle Capitaine (DHAC) said ... deciding what activities to buy and what new service should be delivered was up to the KWHB to decide. If the Board wanted to buy a new service it could....

Marion Scrymgour said the real issue was about lack of control over the clinics ... (and that) the Board was worried about the financial risk in the clinics. The KWHB feels they have no control over nurses ... (and) reiterated her earlier point that if the Board takes over services who is responsible for overexpenditure? Michelle Capitaine said the Board was free to choose, either buy services or provide services.

Mr Little then interrupted this discourse and said he wasn't finished yet. People were asking where the money is going. Mr Patrick

> said that traditional people must be able to see some evidence of change. Mr Little said Board members were getting abused. Marion Scrymgour said staff turnover at the clinics was the biggest problem...
>
> Mr d'Abbs (Evaluator) stated that the structural issues were too big to change in such a short time. Maybe the KWHB should look at undertaking smaller programs. Ms Scrymgour concurred with this ...

And so the arguments went on, back and forth. In this dialogue, there is obviously a mix of answers to Jack's question "When is something going to happen?" Overall, however, the situation reflects the frustration generated by a desire to take on radical initiatives in a context dominated by financial uncertainty and debate about the proper relationship between 'health' and 'community'.

It was true that in theory the Board now had the power to commence new programs—but to do so they were required to start from pre-existing patterns of service delivery and to use planning procedures which had always been the domain of governments rather than community people. When the Board would propose an idea, it was then up to professional staff employed by THS to develop a detailed and costed proposal to implement that idea, and submit the proposal back to the Board for their approval or otherwise. Add to this the fact that Aboriginal people were simply not used to being asked what they thought:

> I've battled this for three years, where I've gone back to those Board members and those community members and said 'Okay, how are we going to do this. You tell me.'

> **But because they're so used to sitting back and having people tell them, it's hard for them to say 'Okay, we want you to do this and this and this.'**
> *(Marion Scrymgour)*

For all these reasons, in this process the issue of who had the real authority became, understandably, a grey area, generating hesitancy on the part of both Board members and THS.

Another significant aspect of this was that, in the early part of the Trial, the administrative practices of THS did little to engender within the KWHB a sense that they had genuine responsibility over the provision of services—THS invoiced KWHB on the basis of a regular monthly charge for the services it had undertaken to provide, rather than on the basis of actual costs incurred in providing such services in a particular month. The KWHB argued strongly that this reduced 'community control' to mere tokenism, and made it impossible to assess whether it was getting 'value for money'.

Subsequently THS did attempt to itemise the services provided on its invoices. Nevertheless, throughout the entire length of the Trial inefficiency in THS' invoicing practices—with late and incorrect invoices being the norm—undermined the ability of KWHB to plan rationally and added enormously to the administrative costs incurred as a huge amount of KWHB staff time had to be spent checking, arguing about and correcting invoices.

And inevitably there were tensions generated by the various personalities involved, heightened by the differing perspectives on power held by Government officers and KWHB people, beautifully illustrated by the desire of the KWHB to retain all copyright over a photo taken by a Canberra-based bureaucrat of the Board's 'Two Roads' poster.

Correspondence via email from OATSIH Canberra to OATSIH Darwin suggested that even though the KWHB may have developed the 'Two Roads to Health Poster' it was Commonwealth money that enabled it and therefore the Commonwealth should be able to do whatever it wanted with it.

Reply email from OATSIH Darwin to OATSIH Canberra challenged this assumption and argued that the times are a changing and maybe it was about time responsiblity for Aboriginal health rested with Aboriginal people rather than bureaucrats in Government.

The tension that arises over issues of ownership reflect the greater underlying issues of control and autonomy. Dynamic processes such as the one that established the KWHB will always unsettle and challenge existing power relationships; even if they become manifest in such seemingly little things like who can reproduce a poster.

In order to generate enthusiasm for Aboriginal people to participate in the KWCCT, great promises had to be made. The reality—at least in the early stages of the Trial—was more prosaic. As time went on and the Board became a service provider in its own right, rather than just purchasing services from others, the pace of change quickened.

Positioning the Health Board

The KWHB was a new organisation in a region where many Aboriginal representative bodies already existed, each of which had a well-defined 'patch'. The challenge for the newly-formed KWHB was to position itself among these bodies in a way which strengthened the overall say which Aboriginal people had in the region yet did not step on the toes of existing organisations. Given the diversity of interests and organisations in the region, a multi-pronged strategy was required.

Among the most influential organisations were the Land Councils and the Local Government Community Councils. The former were established under the Commonwealth Government's *Aboriginal Land Rights (NT) Act 1976*, to represent Aboriginal traditional landowners. The Land Councils have very strong powers over what happens on Aboriginal-owned land in the NT.

The latter were established under the Northern Territory Government's *Local Government Act* to implement basic municipal functions such as power and water services, road maintenance, and so on. Both these sets of bodies had a big say in determining what happened on the ground in communities.

When it moved to directly manage community health centres (clinics), the KWHB set a precedent by applying, through the Northern and Central Land Councils, for leases over those clinics situated on Aboriginal-owned land. This ensured that the KWHB would have 'proper' title to the land and buildings and—more importantly—that traditional Aboriginal landowners would directly give their permission for the KWHB to have a presence in their communities. Before the KWHB came along, when the clinics had been managed by Territory Health Services, no such permission had been sought due to the fact that the NT Government has always been politically opposed to the Land Rights Act.

Next came the relationships with local community councils. The Mid-Term Report of the Local Evaluator had already noted that:

> **Relationships between the Board and community councils are poorly defined, partly because the basis upon which Board**

> members can be said to represent the interests of either community councils or community residents is not clearly defined.

These local councils, usually formed on the basis of elections rather than traditional kinship structures, existed in all the major communities throughout the KWHB region. Where communities are situated on Aboriginal-owned land, local councils have much less power than the Land Councils, but nevertheless do administer many community affairs on a day-to-day basis. And where communities are not situated on Aboriginal-owned land, they have the major say on most issues. Throughout 1998/99 the KWHB negotiated with the local councils in its region to develop Memoranda of Understanding in which they agreed that

- the KWHB would be invited to attend local community council meetings to inform councils of its activities, receive information from councils about issues affecting health and planning, and so on;

- the KWHB would provide the local community councils with relevant documentation and information about KWHB expenditure on health service delivery; and

- the KWHB would invite representatives of the local community councils to attend the periodic meetings of the KWHB.

As with the applications for clinic leases from the Land Trusts, the symbolism of these Memoranda of Understanding was just as important as the substance. They did provide formal documentation of a channel of communication, but also acted in a political sense to position the KWHB as a major player in the affairs of the region.

The final strategic layer wherein the KWHB attempted to gain access to community thinking as it affected health issues, and hence credibility as a community-controlled organisation, was the formation of 'health committees' in all of the major communities in the region. These were informal groupings of residents who were encouraged by the KWHB to meet periodically to raise anything on their minds about which the KWHB should be made aware. The KWHB's Community Development Officer would attend these meetings and relay any matters raised to the KWHB's professional staff. Although these health committees fluctuated in their effectiveness, and required significant amounts of KWHB staff time in order to develop to a functional level, they nevertheless did provide valuable feedback and acted to cement community views that the KWHB did care about what residents thought.

Indigenous Health and Coordinated Care

As pointed out earlier, the Board had decided to 'bite the bullet' and go ahead with the Trial despite their concern that the funds pooled by THS would, most likely, not meet the costs of providing services on the ground.

Having spent the early months of the Live Phase observing the costs of operating the clinics, it became increasingly clear to the Board that the amount pooled by THS would not meet operating costs. The Local Evaluator formally documented this in March 1999, asking the question:

> **Who meets the difference between funds pool and actual expenditure in the event of the KWHB taking over management of ... clinics. If the KWHB is expected to do so out**

> of MBS/PBS cashouts then the latter is, in effect, being used simply to fund a shortfall in basic primary health care services (a State/Territory function) rather than to fund new initiatives—as the terms of the Trial surely envisaged.

This of course had been one of the issues raised by AMSANT in its earlier opposition to the Trial.

It does seem that some within THS were aware of the point that the Health Board had little alternative but to increase resources going to clinical services:

> Our clinics—THS clinics which are now Katherine West clinics—were so under-resourced in the past that it was really critical that they got more. What we were providing was not the wrong service, it was the right service but below the minimum, so they brought these up to the minimum first and then they looked through the public health type-improvements.
> (Jenny Cleary, THS)

This is one aspect of the more general point that some of the preconditions necessary for effective functioning of any primary health care system in remote conditions were not actually present at the commencement of the Katherine West Trial. As the Trial developed, other such 'contextual issues' became increasingly apparent. The Local Evaluator drew specific attention to two of these early on in the Live Phase, labelling them:

(i) 'socio-geographical conditions' such as distance from urban centres and climate. These had such consequences as placing limits on availability of housing, and—most importantly—that telecommunication facilities between far-distant communities lacked the capacity to support the computerised information system (CCTIS) which had been built into the design of the Trial as an essential component. In fact, throughout the entire course of the Trial the CCTIS never did adequately meet the needs of the KWHB.

(ii) 'human resources' issues, such as a chronically high turnover of nursing and management staff, leading to difficulty in Aboriginal Health Workers developing satisfactory working relationships, leading in turn to problems of morale and commitment in the community health centres (though it should be mentioned that turnover and morale improved later in the Trial, as the KWHB came to deliver services directly rather than simply purchasing them from THS).

The key point is that because a variety of these necessary preconditions were not in place before the Trial started, the KWCCT could never be a true test of the value of the concept of 'coordinated care' as originally envisaged.

One important realisation following from this is that Coordinated Care and Indigenous primary health care in remote regions are best seen as conceptually separate issues. As the Local Evaluator pointed out, in terms of the criteria by which the Katherine West Trial should be evaluated,

> **By bringing into the open some of the fundamental requirements of an effective remote area primary health care system, and revealing critical shortfalls by governments in**

meeting these requirements, the Katherine West CCT may help to create the basis for a more effective primary health care system in the future. This, in our judgement, is a potentially more significant outcome than the anticipated short-term achievements of the Coordinated Care Trials as they were originally conceived.
(d'Abbs, 10/12/98)

As it turned out, this is precisely what happened.

Taking Off

By late 1999, the Katherine West Trial was at last in a position to reach its potential. The limitations to the Board's autonomy which were inherent in its role as a purchaser of services from THS had become increasingly apparent; it was time to break the logjam.

Planning documents produced by the KWHB around that time set out a **3-phase strategy**.

Phase 1

The fundamental aim of this Phase was to get the clinics to a state of 'sustainable safety', defined as a situation where a reasonable level of health services would continue to be provided to the community even if the unexpected happened (such as someone going on leave without warning). Employment of GPs based fulltime in communities together with increased numbers of nurses, AHWs and administrative support positions in the clinics formed the main components of this Phase. Phase 2 aimed at increasing the non-clinical public heath services available, with the aim focussed initially on professional environmental health, nutrition, dental and mental health services. Phase 3 proposed the increased employment of community-based Aboriginal trainees in all health service areas, both clinical and non-clinical.

In reality, funding problems intervened to force a reduction in the scope of these plans, but nevertheless significant progress was made.

The first big move came with the progressive takeover of management of the community health centres by the KWHB, commencing in September 1999 and progressing relatively smoothly so that by early 2001 the Health Board was itself providing clinical services in all communities throughout the region—directly employing all staff (GPs, nurses and Aboriginal Health Workers), deciding on health program priorities, implementing programs and managing the health centres.

This itself did a great deal to improve retention of staff in the health centres and encouraged the recruitment of AHWs, as Aboriginal people perceived that their health centre is now a part of the community:

> **In the decade prior to when the Board started to take over management of the clinics, there were only 2 trained Aboriginal Health Workers practising in any of the clinics in the whole Region. By the end of the Trial, there were many more AHWs training, and 3 of the clinics were actually being managed by fully-trained AHWs. One thing which proved successful was that the Board has to approve all new trainees—so the process of selection is now a lengthy one but it makes sure we get the right people, those who've got real commitment.**
> (*KWHB's Aboriginal Health Worker Manager*)

The increased resources on the ground which accompanied the change of management reinforced the value of the KWHB in the eyes of community residents, improving their confidence in the fact that Aboriginal people can achieve real change:

> **Everybody in the community knows it (the health centre) is run by an Aboriginal organisation. It took 30 years to get a doctor based in our community and in this region, and that's a very important step that we've done, to place a doctor there. (Emergency medical) evacuation has dropped a lot lately in those communities in our region, because**

> most people have got a doctor right on site to check them out if they're very sick.
>
> *(Norbert Patrick, KWHB Board member)*

With Board members being present on the ground in communities when a problem arises, they can take a direct interest in its resolution.

> Yeah, they approach me and I try to get it sorted out, try and solve the problem. Or sometimes I go to the clinic—me and that person try and sort it out in the clinic, if it's a big issue. Or, if it gets out of hand, most of the time I ring the office.
>
> *(Norbert Patrick, KWHB Board member)*

It was shown that the combined influence of Board members in the community and senior management in the Katherine office could often resolve conflicts by improving communication between staff and community residents. The 'us and them' thinking which had dominated relations between medical staff and community residents for many years had changed.

> If there's a complaint about a nurse, the first reaction of the Board members or community members now is 'Let's ring the office and talk to the Director and see what needs to be done', and they'll put the complaint this way. Whereas in the past, their reaction was 'Piss off out of our community.'
>
> Or, you know, there'd be a violent incident happening and THS would shut down the clinic, they'd all race out there with their big

> circus, have a meeting with the community which the community didn't fully understand, and THS would fly out of there thinking that they'd done a marvellous job in getting the community to understand why they're shutting the clinic—when the community didn't understand.
>
> It would be good to look over the four years in comparison to before the Trial, the violent incidents that happened pre the Trial versus now, which there's very little.
> *(Marion Scrymgour)*

Phase 2

The next Phase of the Health Board's strategy was that of increasing the level of non-clinical public health services by directly employing its own staff to deal with such specialised areas as nutrition, environmental health, dental services and mental health. As it turned out, adequate funding could not be found and so the plans for fulltime dental and mental health employees had to be shelved. In mid-2000 the KWHB hired a fulltime Nutritionist and a fulltime Environmental Health Officer.

Of course a key rationale behind Phase 2 was the desire by the Board to have more of a say in how these services were implemented. But an equally important reason was the desperate need to increase the absolute level of these services in the region. When the KWHB simply purchased these services from THS, the level of service provided was simply woeful. By way of illustration, for the **3 month** period July–September 1999, the number of days on site (that is, time actually spent in communities) for some of these services purchased from THS were:

- Environmental Health: 6 days approximately
- Nutrition: 8.5 days on site, approximately
- Lifestyle Educator/Disease Control: 6 days on site, approximately
- Hearing: 1 day on site, approximately
- Health Promotion: 8 days on site, approximately

These days on site were for the whole region and hence spread over many communities. The adequacy of these services should be assessed in the context of illness levels many many times those existing in urban centres and of grossly inadequate public health infrastructure and facilities. In this situation, even with the best intentions, it was simply not possible to gain any real momentum in addressing the issues which underlay many clinical presentations.

By contrast, when the KWHB was able to employ its own fulltime Nutritionist and Environmental Health Officer, rather than purchasing these services from THS, the amount of time able to be spent by these people in communities was at least tripled. While still inadequate given the level of need, it was now at least possible to 'get some traction' in implementing community-based programs to address these issues.

Two of the Board members, Roy Harrington and Jack Little, had worked hard on environmental health programs several decades ago but since then there had been little work done, probably because the

> government been too greedy to give out. Otherwise if they could have give out more, we would have been same way, make it better. All those things been happening in past—and Katherine West been pick up all

> those things what can happen now and
> Katherine West been doing it similar.
> *(Jack Little, KWHB Board member)*

These Board members have been unequivocal in emphasising that non-clinical and clinical programs should complement each other:

> Programs like that (environmental health) should tie into one picture with the health. It is a problem out in the community that should be tied into the clinical problem, and meet more needs for Aboriginal health.
> *(Roy Harrington, KWHB Board member)*

> Like with our Environmental Health Officer and Nutritionist, those two. That work may not seem like work for health, but it is. They get you that other side of the (health) picture that normally you don't hear about. You get someone who been knowing all that business in that area, I think it's great. Good.
> *(Brian Pedwell, KWHB Board member)*

The extra volume of these services, plus the increased effectiveness with which they were able to be implemented as a consequence of the involvement of Health Board members and supporters, produced measurable results within a relatively short period, with:

- community-based nutrition interventions associated with significantly decreased levels of childhood anaemia ; and

- a range of community-based environmental health interventions, notably a systematic strategy to tackle the functionality of 'health hardware' in houses, dog control programs in most communities, vermin control programs, etc.

Phase 3

The third Phase of the KWHB's medium-term strategy was to employ increased numbers of community-based Aboriginal Health Worker trainees in both clinical and non-clinical areas. As things turned out, this became less and less of a possibility as funding limitations became critical. Certainly the main bucket of pooled THS and MBS/PBS cashout funds did not adequately allow for this. As a consequence the KWHB looked elsewhere for possible training funds, but largely without success.

Indeed, even finding the money to employ clinic-based AHWs was becoming increasingly difficult. An important aspect of this was that in the view of the KWHB, THS was simply not pooling all that they were required to pool, particularly in regard to AHW positions. A look at the situation at Lajamanu illustrates this well : despite the fact that THS's own organisational chart lists 5 AHW positions as based at the Lajamanu health centre (and that all these positions were filled in the not-distant past), in fact THS only contributed to the funds pool enough money to employ 2 AHWs at Lajamanu! As the KWHB's Medical Director angrily wrote to the NT Minister for Health at the time, at Lajamanu

> **...we have total THS funded staffing capped at little more than half what THS has previously provided, forcing us to use our cashed out MBS/PBS funding to provide services previously funded in full by THS— hence the reason we keep harping on about cost shifting. This is not the intent of the Commonwealth, the Coordinated care Trial model or for that matter of KWHB.**

Whatever the reasons given, the fact remains that despite statements such as 'Strategy Twenty First Century' (1999), 'Aboriginal Public Health Strategy 1997-2002', 'Aboriginal Health Policy' (1996), the 'Preventable Chronic Diseases Strategy' and numerous ministerial and departmental public statements on enhancing and supporting primary care, THS is currently prepared to fund less primary care at Lajamanu than it was five years ago. And that in the face of clearly demonstrated increased need.

<u>What is the point of funding best practice guidelines, expert strategies, innovative information management and recall systems etc etc, if the number of people funded to do the work on the ground in communities has in effect been cut ?</u>

Other Funds, Other Programs

More by luck than planning, between the beginning of 2000 and mid-2001 the KWHB did have success in a number of applications for various grants which were outside of, and conceptually unrelated to, the pooling process of the Coordinated Care Trial. The most significant of these were:

- A grant under the Commonwealth's 'Sharing Health Care' scheme to establish a pilot 'self-management program' at Lajamanu for those with multiple chronic diseases.

- A grant under the Commonwealth's Remote Communities Initiative (RCI) to establish a centre for health promotion activities at Daguragu community, and employ a number of local people to implement community-based health promotion focusing on child nutrition and environmental health issues.

- A grant to meet the operating expenses of the mobile health services visiting the region's cattle stations and the outstations along the WA border.

- A grant to set up a very basic service for aged people in the region, providing meals, laundry services etc to assist old people to remain in their own communities.

These grants were, of course, welcomed by the KWHB. Nevertheless, the fact that it was necessary to search for and apply for separate funding for such programs, under a variety of funding schemes, is at odds with the principles which originally underlay the Coordinated Care Trial. One goal of the 'pooling' principle was to provide an adequate and dependable amount of funds which Indigenous community organisations could then allocate in accordance with their own health priorities. It should have removed the need for community-based organisations to devote valuable staff resources to playing the 'funding game'—searching around for likely schemes, writing submissions, lobbying, and so on. Yet that is the reality of what happened in the Katherine West Trial.

Additionally, during 2001, health services in the KWHB Region benefited from the inclusion of several communities in the ATSIC-Army Community Assistance Program (AACAP). At Yarralin, Lingara and Mialuni (Aminbidji) many new houses were built, sewerage works improved and a range of other construction tasks carried out by the Army. These were of enormous health benefit, and the KWHB frequently provided advice and opinions to the Army on local needs and how things should be done, from a health perspective. The KWHB and the Yarralin community had particularly advocated the need for a separate men's health centre at Yarralin, and benefited from the construction by the Army of such a building, situated on a men's ceremonial area. This shall be the base for the KWHB's mens health program at that community.

So although the original decision to include those communities in the AACAP had not involved the KWHB, by the time the program was implemented the KWHB had developed sufficient capacity to be involved in a fruitful partnership with both the Army and the communities. This acted to increase the utility of the AACAP beyond that which would have been the case if the KWHB had not been responsible for health service provision in the Region.

'Eternal Vigilance'

Close to Anzac Day 2000, the KWHB's Director addressed a conference on the lessons learnt in the Katherine West Trial. The most important, she said, was the need for 'eternal vigilance' when dealing with Governments.

At that time, she had good reason for making that point. THS had been attempting to impose a range of financial penalties on the KWHB, in opposition to both the spirit and letter of the Trial. The issue of pooled funds not meeting the accepted 'establishment' levels of staffing at clinics has been mentioned above. But now more issues arose out of the blue. Although they were strictly financial issues, they nevertheless had to be dealt with on a political level.

At a meeting of the Trial's Monitoring Group on 8 March 2000, the KWHB notified both Governments of a dispute centring on a number of practices of THS as they relate to the funds pool, specifically :

(i) The practice whereby THS does not include 'on costs' in its contribution to the funding pool yet does include such costs in the price of any services purchased from THS. On-costs are defined as the additional costs, other than direct salary, operational and capital costs, incurred when employing staff. In a Position Paper, the KWHB pointed out that

> **In relation to the coordinated care trials, if the Health Board chooses to use additional Commonwealth funding to purchase a new or expanded service from THS, then standard 52% on-costs are charged by THS to KWHB. This is non-negotiable. It is clearly identified in the purchase price of the service. If, however, the Health Board chooses not to purchase 'back' a THS service for which funding was pooled, but to provide it as a community controlled health service provider, then on-costs are not passed on to the Board but are retained by THS.**
> **The apparent but confused logic of the argument made is that while an increase in staffing of, say, one position, increases real costs by 52% of salary, a decrease in staffing of one position does not represent such a saving.**

(ii) The imposition of a 25% surcharge—not matched by an equivalent contribution to the funds pool—on all stores and pharmaceutical drugs purchased from THS by the KWHB. Such pharmaceutical etc purchases were, of course, a consequence of the KWHB taking over management of community health centres (clinics) rather than purchasing such services from THS. The KWHB's Position Paper on this issue pointed out that a key criteria for the cashing out by the Commonwealth of MBS/PBS entitlements was

> agreement by THS to pool to the Health Boards the cost of existing services to the population covered by the Trial ; and to continue to provide at no new or additional cost any services that were provided to this population before the trial for which funds were not pooled. ... This provided protection, from the Commonwealth's perspective, from what was referred to as 'cost shifting'. This would ensure that all cashed out MBS and PBS monies would be available for new services and not replace or fund services previously provided by the NT Government.'

> It is the view of the KWHB that the current attempt to charge the KWHB an additional surcharge of 25% on pharmaceuticals and other supplies is exactly what this arrangement was designed to protect the Health Board and the Commonwealth, as joint funder, from. We see no reason why maintaining the existing supply chain should incur additional cost to THS. The handling of the supply of these items was a service previously provided to these communities by THS for which funds were not pooled, and a service that continues to be provided to THS-managed clinics.

(iii) Inequity in the health service funds provided (and pooled) by THS to the Katherine West region when compared to those funds provided for other regions in the NT. For example, figures presented in December 1999 indicate that the THS contribution to the funds pool for Katherine West on an annual per capita basis were around 67% of that pooled for the Tiwi Region—a shortfall for the Katherine West region of about $1million per annum. This had important implications for the provision of health services. In a letter to the NT Minister for Health, the KWHB's Medical Director pointed out that

> **Correction of the THS underfunding of Katherine West in relation to Tiwi alone would allow the KWHB to proceed with the planned second phase of its program, developing improvements in nutrition, environmental health, dental health, mental health and health promotion.**

The logic of all these issues is inescapable. They were clearly attempts by THS to gain financial advantage, the consequences of which were to make the KWHB spend the Commonwealth's cashed-out MBS/PBS funds on functions which should—according to the original conception of the coordinated care trials—have been funded by THS' contributions to the funds pool. In addressing these issues, the KWHB received no response from correspondence to the NT Minister for Health or by raising them politely at meetings of the Monitoring Group. In the end the KWHB formally requested activation of a clause in the Legal Agreement which provided for the appointment of an independent arbitrator in order to resolve disputes.

With this action, the Commonwealth became sufficiently concerned to place enormous pressure on the NT Government.

Eventually, THS gave way. THS agreed to add an extra 25% to the funds pool to cover the additional charges on pharmaceuticals and stores, to charge and pool the 'genuine' components of 'on costs', and to adjust funding for the various regions across the Top End of the NT. So the KWHB had a victory, of sorts.

But it was not over yet. Not long after these issues had been resolved, THS announced that it intended withdrawing from the funds pool its contributions under the 'Administration and Management' and 'District Medical Officers' categories. Yet again, the KWHB had to go into battle mode—and eventually, after a lot of angry letter-writing and lobbying, THS gave way, agreeing to maintain funds pooling for these functions.

It is important to emphasise two points regarding these disputes.

Firstly, they were disputes which should not have happened if THS had simply stuck to their side of the deal. The division of funding responsibility between the Commonwealth and NT Governments set out in the Coordinated Care Trial proposal, and the rationale behind it, had been clear from the outset. As it turned out, THS had obviously not adequately calculated the extent of their responsibilities, and was not comfortable with their financial commitment. This goes back to a key point made earlier in this story: that the Coordinated Care Trial turned out to be less a means of assessing the value of 'coordinated care' and more of a way to illustrate and assess the true costs of maintaining a primary health care service for Aboriginal people in remote areas—of establishing the 'essential preconditions' necessary to even begin to assess coordinated care as a concept.

Secondly, in arguing against these financial discrepancies, the KWHB had to utilise a great deal of resources, particularly human resources. Highly paid senior staff devoted a lot of time to writing position papers, letters and other policy documents, attending meetings, and lobbying key bureaucrats and advisors in order to effectively press their case. At times they even had to issue media releases and appear on public radio etc. While all this comes under the notional heading of 'advocacy', and as such is legitimate activity for an Aboriginal health service, it is nevertheless a function for which the KWHB was not specifically funded. In this sense, KWHB resources which could have been better used to plan and deliver health services were diverted to other functions.

But Marion and the Board did appreciate an important lesson from all this: that 'constant vigilance' was indeed necessary when dealing with Governments.

Not that some people—particularly old Jack Little—hadn't been saying this from the beginning, of course.

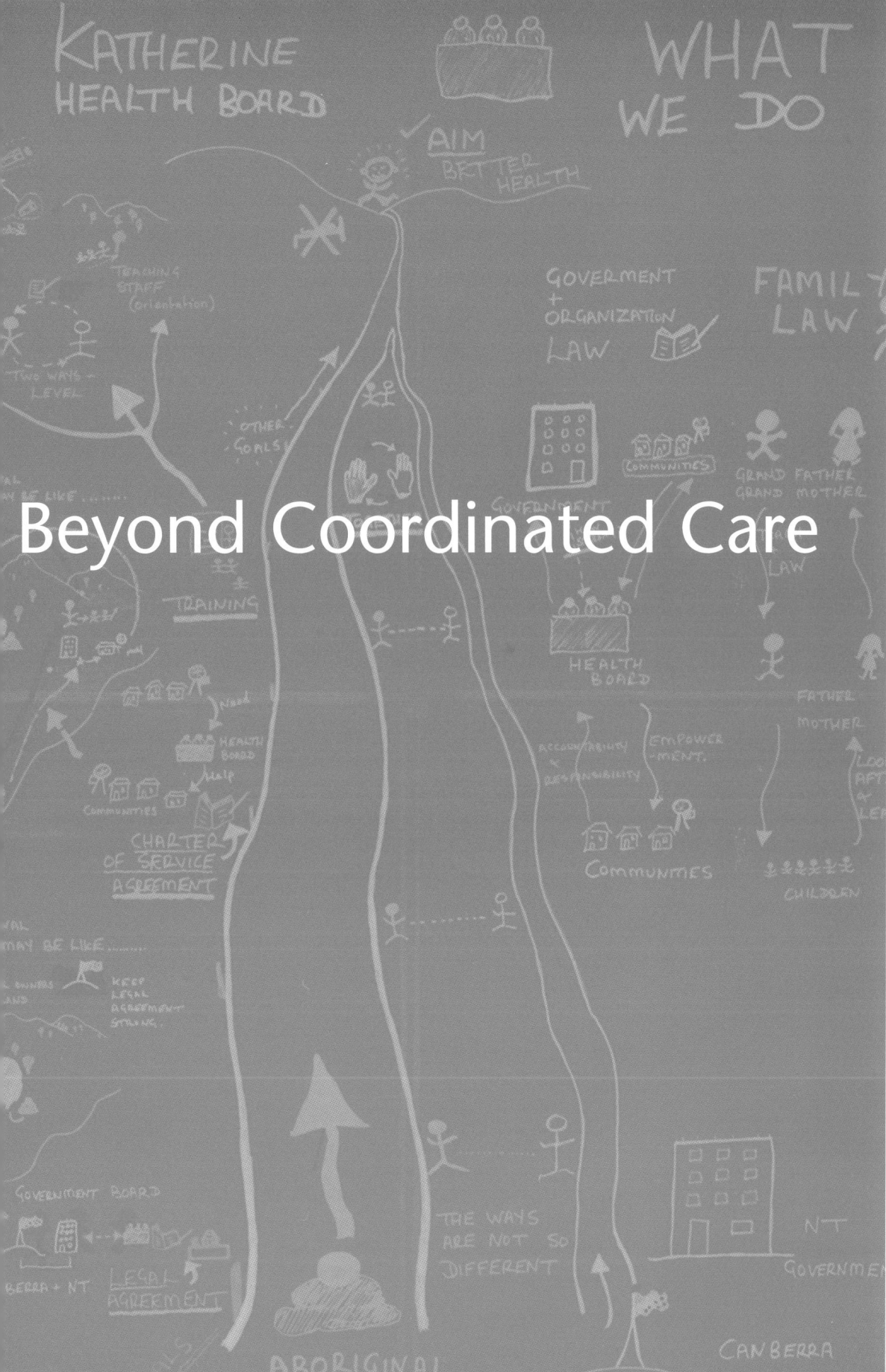

Beyond Coordinated Care

The Katherine West Trial officially came to an end in late-2001. In a letter to the KWHB's Chairman, the Commonwealth Minister for Health said

> **I believe that the success of the Katherine West Trial provides a sound base for meeting challenges that lie ahead, and our continuing partnership with the Katherine West Health Board and NT Government will build on these achievements and progress the reforms.**

The lessons to be drawn from the Katherine West experience vary according to one's perspective—of course ! Some of them were documented in Evaluation Reports, others were less formally set out. The Minister had based his letter on the conclusions of the National Evaluation of the Aboriginal Coordinated Care Trials.

The National Evaluation

The main arbiter of success from an official viewpoint was the Report of the National Evaluation of the Aboriginal Coordinated Care Trials. This National Evaluation had used the criteria of:

- access to health services
- appropriateness of services
- organisational capacity
- funding and administrative arrangements
- empowerment of individuals
- empowerment of communities

to reach the conclusion that:

> The trials demonstrated that the effectiveness of good clinical, public health, administrative and financial practice can be realised if the reform agenda is driven through community organisations that are adequately resourced and supported. Irrespective of the amount of (additional) resources, the trials also demonstrated that account must be taken of the time required for organisations to build that capacity.

This is little more than a confirmation of what the Aboriginal community-controlled health sector in the NT had been asserting for some years, and it is difficult to see how such a generalisation can be used as a guide to precise policy decisions. Nevertheless, Canberra no doubt felt that this conclusion justified the expense and risks it had undertaken in establishing the Aboriginal Trials. And the Commonwealth *had* taken risks, primarily in the form of the unprecedented cashout of MBS/PBS entitlements :

> The NT was getting heaps out of the coordinated care trials, because we'd been bleating to the Commonwealth for ever about 'the NT doesn't get enough money to make up for the lack of access to Medicare and blah blah blah' and Coordinated Care Trials was the vehicle on which we were pinning our hopes for that. So we were actually getting heaps out of the Trials, whereas the Commonwealth was taking on risks, but I don't think they could really see

> **the size of the payoffs that were going to come, and I still don't think they see them.**
> *(Jenny Cleary, THS)*

So from an official viewpoint the Trial showed that an injection of extra cash into health services in remote regions with high morbidity was needed, and could produce good results. The MBS/PBS cashout 'experiment' had been justified.

The National Evaluation also offered confirmation of some other important experiences which the Board had been through over the course of the Trial. In particular, the emphasis on the need to <u>build capacity</u> had been seen as vital. In the case of Katherine West, this had taken two main forms:

- A long leadup period to allow for extensive community consultations, discussion and debate. This goes beyond the usual way in which governments define 'consultations'—such as just having one or two meetings and talking to a half dozen people or local councils. Instead, in the Katherine West experience 'consulting' meant that virtually every adult in each of the communities concerned had to be made aware of the proposal—through face to face discussions—then given time to reflect upon the implications, their opinions sought, the original proposal revised in light of this, and so on. It required nothing less than detailed individual dialogue, which was ongoing throughout all phases of the Trial and could not be fitted into timetables dictated by the program funding cycles which emanated from Canberra:

  > **There was pressure from the Commonwealth in terms of programs happening, saying 'Still nothing's happening, what's going on ?'. And we kept saying 'The foundations—even though you people see things in neat little**

> boxes—even though we're in the Live Phase, we're still developing what should have been given more time back here. Sure, we're purchasing services based on the funding pool, but in terms of community programs and what's happening out there, none of that's going to happen until further down the track. The Board needs to lay that strong foundation in the communities. Consultations will continue.'
> (Marion Scrymgour)

- The empowerment of Board members which is inherent in a comprehensive training program. The 'Money Story' was a key aspect of this but it went beyond the explanation of an accounting system—to be genuinely empowering it had to go to the *cultural meanings* of money. Because the training, to be successful, had to be based on dealing with real problems, it could not be neatly 'packaged' into a limited session but instead became an integral component of every meeting. In the process it branched out into a means to help Board members deal with decisions relating to such issues as conflicts of interest, constitutions, contracts and so on—a cultural mediation process around the twin issues of

> Money, and responsibility. Given over to us. To run our affairs with our own Aboriginal people. Because we know what's happening out there with our own people, which it's harder to know what's going on. Money and responsibility.
> (Willie Johnson, KWHB Board member)

> **They (governments) been watching us like a hawk. Because a lot of money been put toward Katherine West. They probably thought we might waste it away for some other things that it's not suitable for. But we been really careful with that money to make things happen. And we have been really open our eyes to see where's our money go, in what, how much in our budget—things like that.**
> *(Jack Little, KWHB Board member)*

It is worth noting that although the National Evaluation eventually recognised the importance of these two aspects of capacity-building, neither was given sufficient importance by the Governments *at the time*. There was no allowance provided for 'training' in the original budgets, and the timetables set for the Trial were rigid and largely unrelated to the perceived readiness of communities to participate.

In the Eyes of the Board

The National Evaluation Report documented the Katherine West Trial from the perspective of the accounting firm which wrote it, for the Commonwealth Government which commissioned it. As such it told only a part of the story.

Although only part of the story, for the Board members themselves it was nevertheless a useful part—official recognition from such non-Aboriginal sources that the Trial had been a 'success' was a mark of their achievement. The Board members were gratified to know that non-Aboriginal society now saw that Aboriginal people could do things for themselves:

> **Most of the stuff that we've take over through this organisation, we done it right in front of the non-Aboriginal people's eyes, and they know very well—really—that we're making an effort for our own people who are this organisation.**
> *(Norbert Patrick, KWHB Board member)*

There is no doubt that Board members went through a great deal of personal growth as a consequence of the KWHB experience. Time and again Board members emphasised this when interviewed for this study:

> **It wasn't until in the meetings, coming in here and listening to all the facts about how important our health out there—what are the problems—you don't know anything about what's the problems out there until you come in here and you're hit ...**
> *(Brian Pedwell, KWHB Board member)*

> **From my inner man, whatever thing been happening in the past, and everything that I have done with Marion and others about what sort of work we want to do, has sort of strengthened me...**
> *(Jack Little, KWHB Board member)*

Testing the thesis

On a key issue, however, the Katherine West Trial did not ultimately prove (or disprove) one of its primary theses—that is, the utility of the concept of 'coordinated care'. As detailed earlier, the absence of some of the necessary preconditions for this—stable and adequate staffing, a smoothly functioning IT system, and other contextual factors—inhibited the ability of the Katherine West Trial to seriously test the usefulness of coordinated care as *originally envisaged*. This testing may yet happen, of course, but if so it will be beyond the time confines of the Trial.

The need to ensure the establishment of such preconditions in advance if one wants to test the concept is itself, of course, a major lesson learnt by the KWHB. As things turned out, the principle whereby THS contributed the funds which it would otherwise have spent on delivering primary health care in the region did not take into account of the fact that such services—as they were actually delivered prior to the Trial—were themselves inadequate. Because of this, it was necessary to spend a portion of the Commonwealth's cashed-out MBS/PBS funds to bring the basic service delivery up to even a minimally-adequate level.

A similar point applies in regard to the funds necessary to manage and administer health services. The small amounts contributed to the funds pool by both THS and the Commonwealth for such administration/management purposes was inadequate throughout the length of the Trial. It was necessary during the Trial to set up a central office for the KWHB in Katherine, to employ administrative staff, to purchase computers, pay rent, maintain accounts, lease and service vehicles, pay the travel and accommodation expenses of Board members when they attended meetings in Katherine, to pay for travel and accommodation expenses of senior staff and Board members when they were required to attended numerous meetings with Governments in Darwin, and so on. As a consequence, some of the cashed-out MBS/PBS funds had to be spent on these administrative functions rather than specifically on health programs. This point was made repeatedly by the KWHB to both Governments throughout the Trial, but without response.

The Director and the Board

Apart from the above issues, perhaps the most important lessons from the Trial revolved around qualitative, rather than quantitative, matters - which were harder for the accounting firm which carried out the National Evaluation to pin down. They are concerned with the *quality of relationships* between the various players. This study has commented already on the shifting relationship between the Board and Governments, as each dealt with new situations and defined new relationships. Pre-eminent among the other key relationships was that existing between the Director and members of the Board.

In analysing the factors which led to the success of the KWCCT, it is difficult to overstate the importance of the quality of the relationship between the Director and the Board.

> **When we saw Marion, we didn't look at her colour—we look at her.**
> *(Jack Little)*

The trust between the Board members and the Director was apparent from the start—and it developed for reasons of political commitment: because they were involved in the one struggle together. Their commitment was mutually reinforcing.

> **Marion was really good when we started our program up. She was really strong on it, she really felt for the Aboriginal people about our health, and she really supported you right up.**
> *(Roy Harrington, KWHB Board member)*

> **There is something in Marion that brings out the best in you—words can't explain this. She committed herself—commitment is the main thing.**
> (Joseph Cox, KWHB Board member)

Throughout the Trial, the Director was the most important channel of communication to Board members and from Board members. This was sometimes controversial, but there was no doubting its truth. Its rationale was both practical and political:

> **Some people couldn't understand that my role was gatekeeper. So the Board members didn't get burnt out at meetings, I had to screen all that information going to them, and try and weigh up and determine what was going to be the right information—so that information would be abosrbed, rather than bogging the members down with a hundred and one other things which were going to be meaningless and didn't have any relevance to them on the ground in the community. And that was a constant frustration for managers and governments, to understand that they couldn't get to those Board members until they went through me.**
>
> **But that was for a reason. Much as I pushed those Board members and played advocate, I also had to nurture them and make sure that their information overload didn't burn them out. And we did lose a lot of young Board**

> members, because they were scared, they were frightened from the amount of information that was hitting the Board. And because their confidence was down, they felt inadequate in themselves, thinking 'I can't do this. I'm not able to understand.'
>
> So that was the gatekeeper role I had to play, it was the most important one—the information had to be streamlined and made simple so they didn't overload.
>
> The important aspect of being a gatekeeper is sorting out delegations. Roles and responsibilities of your top people. If the Director has the delegations written very clearly in black and white, and approved by the Board, there's a lot of things that don't have to go to the Board, that the Director has powers to deal with. The thing with that where it can be dangerous, and where I was very conscious, was that every decision I'd taken in the organisation was always taken back to the Board so that they weren't excluded from the process.
> (*Marion Scrymgour*)

In maintaining the commitment of Board members, it is difficult to overestimate the importance of the quality of communication apparent during Board meetings. Unlike the meetings of many Aboriginal bureaucracies, in KWHB meetings the Board members *understood* what was happening. This understanding underlay their commitment.

A partial reason behind the effectiveness of such communication was the role played by 'training' described above. Another partial reason was the role played by the Director and in managing the information flow, particularly to the Chairperson:

> **(At meetings) we go through our Chairperson, and some of our Chairperson like me for instance cannot read the government words. That's the reason we have to put it back to Marion so he knows how to speak, and he knows the system and he got the ideas because he been working with the government department for a long time, and when she usually come and talk to us about all these things. And we throw all these ideas up in the air, and that's what happens, (we say) 'Alright we go that way'.**
> *(Jack Little, KWHB Board member)*

The point is that involvement and commitment of Board members is an outcome of the clarity of understanding, and in this the communication skills of the Director were crucial:

> **We would go to the Board meetings and Marion was really clear about it—being the needs and health problems in our communities, she used to bring it real clear. We could understand it and we could know what to say. It's a lot different to ATSIC meetings—it is more clear what is really spent and what money is really coming to you and that.**
> *(Roy Harrington, KWHB Board member)*

And what of Marion herself? Is there a role for a troublemaker?

> You know, one of the biggest lessons that I was wanting the Commonwealth and Northern Territory (Governments) to learn—and I certainly think those members took it on board—was that for a lot of people like me that go to work in organisations, some Commonwealth officers and Territory officers saw someone like me as being a little activist and just a shitstirrer. I saw myself as being advocate rather than an activist, and there's big difference between an advocate and an activist.

(Marion Scrymgour)

What now?

Much remains to be done.

In terms of future direction, all Board members interviewed for this study were adamant that the KWHB's future expansion needs to take place not inside the health centres but outside, in the communities at large. The debate about 'clinic versus community' has gone on throughout the life of the Trial, with Board members emphasising from the very start that:

> we need programs in the communities. The problems lie in the communities, not lie in the clinics

(Joseph Cox, KWHB Board member)

This has not yet been achieved. In an ideal situation, of course, there is a need for both clinical *and* community-based services.

This point is appreciated by senior staff, but its implementation faces the twin barriers of resource availability and the habit of working in situations where one is comfortable, as the KWHB's Medical Director points out:

> **I think our staff do need to do a lot more work outside the clinic. And that's part of being seen in the community. Although people feel more comfortable with being in the clinic, it creates a boundary. One of the issues we still face is the resources we're going to need, and that's part of the reason why it's hard to provide a holistic model of health care.**

The KWHB was bound by the terms of the Trial to prioritise clinical care, and this difficult issue reflects more than historical patterns of service provision—it also reflects the reality of scarce resources in the face of huge potential demand. With the Trial now officially finished, the need remains to integrate the 'inside-clinic' and 'outside-clinic aspects of health care. In this process, the issue of whose *values* to use when allocating resources remains relevant.

Another major task yet to be seriously tackled is establishing a genuine understanding of Aboriginal culture within the non-Aboriginal staff of the KWHB. The training of Board members in such whitefella systems as accounts, contracts and so on is one thing. But the training of non-Aboriginal staff in Aboriginal ways is another, and remains largely to be implemented at Katherine West. It is, however, important.

> **You know, we've hit the Board with training, and we've hit the Board with getting them to understand health, but we've neglected**

> the (staff) who are supposed to be projecting that to them. We think (staff) have a certain level of skill. One of the skills they don't have is getting that program and then implementing it on the ground in the community. The hardest concept is to implement health in a community development framework. And a lot of them don't know how to do it. I was observing a (recent) Board meeting, with (a senior staff member) talking to the Board. Nearly every session I had with the Board after that, not one of them understood what he had been talking about.
>
> Now if the interpretation and communication isn't clear to them, how does he expect them to grab this project and be enthusiastic about it ? How do you grab that information and make it exciting?
> *(Marion Scrymgour)*

Even beyond the matter of effective communication in such formal settings as Board meetings, however, is the need to establish common ground between Aboriginal and non-Aboriginal constructions of illness and causation. This was never a goal of the Coordinated Care Trials, and hence the approach of the KWHB has been based on conventional epidemiological concepts. Yet from the traumatic history of Katherine West region there can be little doubt that spiritual damage is widespread and that spiritual recovery is necessary. The issue of how to carry this out remains largely outside a western scientific discourse, yet any Aboriginal health service cannot ignore the implications of the dictum that

> When people and country are *punyu* life is nurtured, and both remain strong, healthy and fruitful.
> *(Rose 2000, p.68)*

The causal connection between good health of people and country on the one hand, and harmonious social relations on the other—summarised in the above statement—remains a topic yet to be seriously explored by the KWHB.

Allied to this is the need for the KWHB to be involved—at *some* level at least—in strategies for the Region's overall socioeconomic development. The control by Aboriginal people of their own health service is just one aspect of the development of models of Indigenous social control. Other aspects, no less important, focus on the need to find sustainable economic activities which can provide an alternative to the current reliance on welfare payments from the Government. This seems as far away as ever, but the need is undeniable, as is the link between useful employment and health status.

> **No economically viable alternative to employment in the pastoral industry (itself now struggling and with an uncertain future in the Region) has emerged for the Aboriginal population. The notion of full—if inadequately remunerated—employment has become something of a mocking illusion from the past for the generations that have grown up in the shadow of Vincent Lingiari and has surviving contemporaries ... An Aboriginal economy which can marry Aboriginal notions of resource use, kinship**

> **and work roles with the need to relate to the priorities of late twentieth century Australia, in a way which emphasises respect and equality of outcomes, is yet to be developed.**
> *(Katherine West Health Board, October 1999)*

So, important things remain to be done. Nevertheless, the viability of the Board and of the whole Katherine West 'experiment' had been proven beyond doubt.

The completion of the Katherine West Trial coincided with the commencement of a major funding program for the planned expansion of Indigenous community-controlled heath care services in the Northern Territory, titled the Primary Health Care Access Program, or PHCAP. Under the PHCAP, the Commonwealth would provide funding to such services equivalent to a multiple of the Australian MBS usage rate. So in a way the cashout of MBS/PBS entitlements which was a core feature of the Katherine West Trial had been superseded by a more innovative long-term scheme.

The KWHB was to be included in the PHCAP arrangements and so will now have a long-term future. A future which—unlike the past—can be based on *equity and reciprocity* between black and white throughout the region, where Aboriginal people can expect

> **that their words will connect with those of others, that others will recognise the key events and find their own strong stories which, as they implement them in their own lives and places, will answer back in affirmation.**
> *(Rose 2000, p. 234/5)*

References

Berndt R and Berndt C (1987), *End of an Era: Aboriginal Labour in the Northern Territory*, Australian Institute of Aboriginal Studies, Canberra.

d'Abbs P (10/12/98), 'Issues associated with the implementation of the Katherine West Coordinated Care Trial: a Discussion Paper'. Unpublished.

d'Abbs P, Togni S et al (April 2000), *Jirntangku Miyrta Katherine West Coordinated Care Trial. Final Report*, Menzies School of Health Research, Darwin.

Deeble J (1998), *Expenditures on Health Services for Aboriginal and Torres Strait Islander People*, Australian Institute for Health and Welfare and National Centre for Epidemiology and Population Health, Canberra.

Doolan J (1977), 'Walk-off (and later return) of various Aboriginal groups from cattle stations : Victoria River District, Northern Territory, in Berndt R (ed.), *Aborigines and Change: Australia in the 70s*, Australian Institute of Aboriginal Studies, Canberra.

Hardy F (1976), *The Unlucky Australians*, Rigby.

Katherine West Health Board (October 1999), *Year 2000 and Beyond : A Submission in Relation to Short Term and Medium Term Development Strategies*, KWHB (unpublished).

Kettle E (1991), *Health Services in the Northern Territory – A History 1824-1970*, Volumes 1 and 2, North Australian Research Unit, Australian National University, Darwin.

Northern Land Council (1979), *Yingawunarri (Old Top Springs) Mudbura Land Claim*, NLC, Darwin.

Northern Land Council (1984), *Timber Creek Land Claim*, NLC, Darwin.

Northern Land Council (1987), *Historical Submission. Aminbidji Land Claim (Draft)*, unpublished.

Read P and Japaljarri EJ, 'The price of tobacco : the journey of the Warlmala to Wave Hill, 1928', *Aboriginal History*, 1978, 2: 2.

Rose, Deborah Bird (1991), *Hidden Histories. Black Histories From Victoria River Downs, Humbert River and Wave Hill Stations*, Aboriginal Studies Press, Canberra.

Rose, Deborah Bird (2000), *Dingo Makes Us Human. Life and Land in an Australian Aboriginal Culture*, Cambridge University Press, Cambridge.

Riddett,Lyn A (1988), Kine, Kin and Country : The Victoria River District of the Northern Territory 1911–1966, Thesis submitted for Doctorate of Philosophy Degree, Department of History, James Cook University of North Queensland.

Example : funding and service delivery mechanisms in the 'Katherine West' region before the CC Trial:

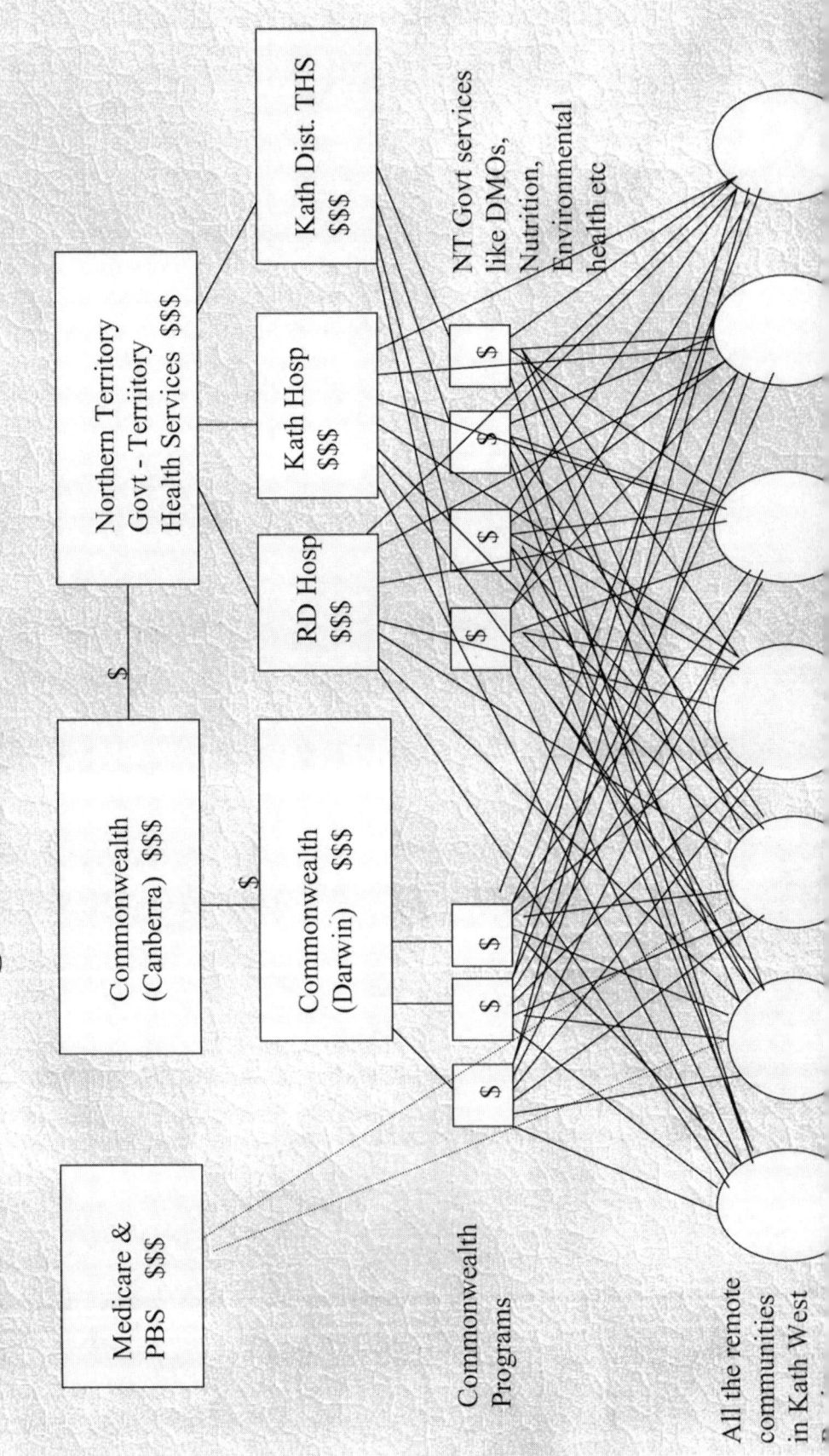